I0191922

Directors of Convict Prisons

Directors of Convict Prisons in Ireland : twenty-first annual report,

1874

Directors of Convict Prisons

Directors of Convict Prisons in Ireland : twenty-first annual report, 1874

ISBN/EAN: 9783741105241

Manufactured in Europe, USA, Canada, Australia, Japa

Cover: Foto ©ninafisch / pixelio.de

Manufactured and distributed by brebook publishing software
(www.brebook.com)

Directors of Convict Prisons

Directors of Convict Prisons in Ireland : twenty-first annual report,

1874

TWENTY-FIRST ANNUAL REPORT

OF THE

DIRECTOR OF CONVICT PRISONS

FOR IRELAND,

FOR THE YEAR ENDED 31st DECEMBER,

1874;

WITH APPENDIX.

Presented to both Houses of Parliament by Command of Her Majesty.

DUBLIN:

PRINTED BY ALEXANDER THOM, 87 & 88, ABBEY-STREET,

FOR HER MAJESTY'S STATIONERY OFFICE.

1875.

[C.—1220.] *Price 3½d.*

TABLE OF CONTENTS.

TWENTY-FIRST ANNUAL REPORT

OF THE

DIRECTOR OF CONVICT PRISONS

FOR IRELAND,

UNDER 17 & 18 VIC., CAP. 76.

TO THE RIGHT HON. SIR M. E. HICKS BEACH, BART., M.P.,

CHIEF SECRETARY FOR IRELAND.

Government Prisons Office, Dublin Castle,
April, 1875.

SIR,

In accordance with the provisions of the Act 17 & 18 Vic., cap. 76, I beg to submit the Annual Report on the state of the Convict Prisons in Ireland for 1874.

Accommodation.

The accommodation for convicts in the Government Prisons on the 1st January, 1875, may be estimated as amounting to 1,670.

GOVERNMENT PRISONS.

	Males.	Females.	Total.
Number in custody 1st January, 1875,	852	281	1,133
Accommodation 1st January, 1875,	1,274	396	1,670

COUNTY AND CITY GAOLS.

	Males.	Females.	Total.
Number in custody 1st January, 1875,	3	1	4

Gross Total of Convicts in Ireland, 1,137.

NUMBER OF CONVICTS SENTENCED TO PENAL SERVITUDE DURING THE YEAR 1874.

	Males.	Females.	Total.
5 years,	94	35	129
7 ,,	53	22	75
8 ,,	2	–	2
10 ,,	9	1	10
14 ,,	2	–	2
Life,	1	2	3
Gross Total sentenced in 1874,	161	60	*221

DISPOSAL OF CONVICTS.

Discharged unconditionally, on completion of sentence, &c.,	55
Released on Orders of Licence,	174
Total,	229

* Six of these are military convicts.

The Revocations of Licences during the year 1874 were as follow :—

Males—

Forfeited and revoked for breach of conditions, .   6*

    „   for new offences, ...   6

Females—

Revoked for breach of conditions in Refuges, &c.,   10

    „   for new offences, ...   4

Subjoined is a table similar to that given in previous Annual Reports, showing the number of Convicts respectively "In Custody," &c., "Convicted," and "Discharged," since the year 1854, inclusive—

In custody in Government Prisons, January 1st.	Year.	Convicted.	No. Discharged.
†3,933	1854	710	658
3,427	1855	518	820
3,209	1856	389	1,107
2,614	1857	426	910
2,277	1858	358	946
1,773	1859	322	595
1,631	1860	331	524
1,492	1861	388	561
1,314	1862	592	317
1,575	1863	511	326
1,768	1864	407	341
1,776	1865	299	410
1,637	1866	265	439
1,431	1867	296	330
1,335	1868	246	245
1,325	1869	191	291
1,230	1870	245	253
1,228	1871	219	265
1,195	1872	201	255
1,143	1873	228	250
1,133	1874	‡229	229
1,133	1875		

No material change has taken place during the past year in the Irish Convict Service, with the exception of the retirement of the Inspector, the Honorable Mr. Netterville, whose office was abolished. Mr. Netterville had served for many years in this Department as Governor of Mountjoy Male Convict Prison and subsequently as Inspector. I much regret his retirement, having served for many years with him, and been invariably afforded every assistance by him. The numbers of convicts in custody on the 31st of December, 1874, were exactly the same as those in custody on the 31st of December, 1873. Owing, however, to prisoners having been in many instances sentenced to more lengthened periods of penal servitude, I do not believe any decrease in the numbers of convicts is for some years to be

* One was an English licence holder.

† In addition to this number there were 345 convicts under detention in the county prisons, and several hundred in Bermuda and Gibraltar, who were subsequently discharged in Ireland.

‡ Six of these are military convicts.

expected. In the Prisons for Male Convicts, nothing requiring special remark occurred during the past year, the conduct of the prisoners having been generally satisfactory, some cases of violence and persistent misconduct rendered corporal punishment in some few instances unavoidable. Having due regard to the safety of the Prison officers, and also to protect convicts from violence from their fellow-prisoners, it is not possible to avoid this mode of punishment. In the Mountjoy Female Prison, in September last, a disposition to violence became so marked, that I found it necessary to report specially to you on the subject, the entire staff were by His Grace the Lord Lieutenant's order, gravely cautioned as to their future conduct, no doubt there were some officers who faithfully and firmly did their duty, but should any such misconduct unchecked and unreported again occur, it will become my duty to recommend, with some few exceptions, an entire change in the discipline staff of this Prison, some changes already made, and some which will be made during the present year, will, I trust, prevent the recurrence of any similar misconduct on the part of the convicts. The prison is now working satisfactorily, and with fewer cases of punishment. I regret to have to make these remarks, but if misconduct and irregularities on the part of officers and prisoners are not reported, it is simply impossible, more especially in a female Convict Prison, for anyone holding my position to maintain discipline, and to ensure to well-conducted officers and to prisoners the benefits which should in either case result to officers who do their duty, and to prisoners who endeavour by their good conduct to obtain the advantages to which they are entitled by the rules laid down by the Government.

With the exceptions I have mentioned, the general conduct of the officers of the Convict Service has been extremely good. The duties of Prison officials are at all times harassing, often dangerous; it is not going too far to remark, that they probably of all Civil Servants, have no relief, excepting during absence on leave, from continuous anxiety. I trust, that if possible, officers of all ranks in the Convict Service, may be placed as far as regards retirement, on as good terms as officials in County Prisons, who are not exposed to the same danger as officers in charge of convicts.

The health of the officers and of the convicts has been very good.

The usual reports from the Governors, Superintendents, Chaplains, Medical Officers, and Teachers in the Schools, are attached.

I may be permitted to remark as to the expenditure of the Department, which has been very unfavourably commented upon, doubtless, in ignorance of the real facts of the case. The Male and Female Convict Prisons at Mountjoy, and Lusk Prison, are more than half empty, it is necessary even if still fewer convicts were located there, to keep up all the more expensive portions of the staff of these Prisons, with small numbers contracts cannot be made as advantageously as with larger numbers, hence, sources of increased expense which cannot be avoided. Spike Island

Prison, originally a military barrack, and adapted as well as circumstances admit for Prison purposes, requires from the insecure nature of the buildings, and also from its insular situation a staff of nearly one-third more than would be necessary in a properly constructed Prison, and here again, contracts are higher than they would be in a Prison situated in a more accessible situation. The Prisons are all situated in two of the most expensive localities in Ireland, Dublin and Queenstown.

I have in previous reports referred to the cost of repairs and the supply of fuel and light being under the control of the Royal Engineer Department and the Board of Works. This to a great extent renders the employment of convicts difficult, and entails, in my opinion, very unnecessary expense, besides introducing amongst the convicts free labour, an objectionable practice in every point of view.

A properly-constructed prison in lieu of Spike Island, and the restoration to their proper use as barracks of the Spike Island buildings, would I believe result in a large saving to the public. The erection of such a prison in a locality where some works for public benefit would for many years to come occupy the convicts would be of much advantage, not only to the public but to convicts, whose labour could be utilized much more were their employment placed under the control of the Prison Department, in place of as at present being under the control of other departments where convicts are worked to some extent with free labourers, and where the Prison Department cannot be made, as it should be, responsible for a proper amount of labour being performed.

The employments of the convicts have been much the same as in former years. The Admiralty have employed the majority of the convicts located at Spike Island at the Haulbowline Docks; for some time, however, they have not required the full number whose labour could have been afforded. The convicts not so required have been employed at Spike Island by the Royal Engineer Department.

It is satisfactory to be able to report that during the past two years the number of cases of re-convictions have largely decreased. I have every reason to believe that this is not owing to discharged prisoners having left this country to a greater extent than in former years, but to the fact that very many are earning an honest livelihood, and also that convicts find on their re-conviction and return to a convict prison that they are not as a convenience employed at trades or placed in the easy position, comparatively speaking, which exists in all prisons where prisoners' labour is as far as may be utilized. I have again to report as to the great advantages which result from the Refuges to which the well-conducted female convicts are transferred before release on licences to be at large, especially to Golden Bridge Refuge, which is exclusively for Roman Catholic convicts; the small numbers of Protestant and Presbyterian prisoners render it almost impossible to support a refuge exclusively for such cases. To Golden Bridge is, I believe, owing the marked diminution in the number of female convicts in Ireland.

In cases where convicts released on licence fail to comply with the conditions of their licences, it is to be regretted that magistrates in many instances pass over such cases with a caution. I believe that when released convicts endeavour to evade the conditions of their licence they are without exception of a most dangerous class to the public. In all such cases, so far as I can judge, if the breach of conditions of licence were proved, a conviction should be compulsory, leaving the Government to decide whether the penalty should be carried out or otherwise.

As Registrar of Habitual Criminals it may not be out of place here to remark, that I believe all cases of prisoners under Police Supervision, who fail to report themselves should involve the full penalty, leaving it as before suggested, to the Government to deal with any cases in which a remission might be considered just; as remarked in a former report, much judgment and consideration for convicts on licence and prisoners under Police Supervision, has been invariably shown by the Royal Irish Constabulary, the Metropolitan Police, and the Police in England; and as a protection not only to the Public, but to the criminal classes themselves, it is much to be regretted that a penalty so much dreaded, so effectual and lastly so economical, is not more frequently resorted to. Amongst the cases sent to the Office of Registrar of Habitual Criminals, are many of soldiers convicted by the Civil power, the crimes having been apparently committed with the view of being discharged from the Army, such crimes are not committed through poverty, if some kind of Police Supervision could be ordered in these cases, it is not improbable that such a source of petty crime would much decrease.

I have the honour to be,

Sir,

Your obedient servant,

J. BARLOW.

MOUNTJOY MALE CONVICT PRISON.

On the 31st of March, 1874, a considerable reduction in number
of the staff of this prison, recommended by me in the previous
year, took place; the reductions amounted to one-fourth of the
existing staff. I do not believe any further reduction can be
made, having due regard to the safety of the prison, and mainte-
nance of proper discipline.

The conduct of the subordinate officers has been satisfactory.

During the past year 187 convicts were received, 189 were
transferred to Spike Island and Lusk Prisons, 11 were discharged,
and 1 death occurred.

The health of the prisoners has been good.

No change in the arrangements of the prison or in the employment of the convicts has taken place.

The general conduct of the convicts has been good, they were
industrious and attentive to the work in which they have been
employed.

The usual reports from the prison officials, with statistics, are
attached.

J. BARLOW, Director.

GOVERNOR'S REPORT.

Mountjoy Male Convict Prison,
January, 1875.

SIR,—I have the honour to submit my annual report with the
statistical returns of this prison for the year ending 31st December,
1874.

There has been a considerable reduction in the number of the staff of
the prison since my last report. Eleven officers less, including a chief
clerk and assistant schoolmaster, than were employed under the estimates
1873–74 are now doing duty here. This makes a reduction of one-fourth
of the then existing staff.

It is gratifying for me to be able to report that in proportion to the
number of the staff, the pay of the remaining staff who have been left to
do duty in the prison has been increased, with one or two exceptions, and
that a feeling of satisfaction is manifested at the present scale of pay.

The conduct of the subordinate officers during the past twelve months
has been very good. There has been no case of dismissal, nor have any
serious reports been made against any member of the staff within that
period.

I have been well and cordially supported by the entire staff of the
prison throughout the year, and the superior and subordinate officers
have in every way helped by zeal and attention to meet and perform the
duties which were necessarily increased by the heavy reduction of the
staff.

The labour of the prisoners continues to be utilized as heretofore in the making of mats, matting, the manufacture of ship-fendoffs, and the usual penal employment of oakum-picking. A slackness in the demand of mats, &c., induced me to ease the work in the manufacturing department during some portions of the year, in order that too heavy a stock of manufactured articles might not remain on hands at the close of the year, and cause an accumulation which would perhaps hereafter oblige a forced sale and pecuniary loss to the department. MOUNTJOY MALE CONVICT PRISON. *Governor's Report.*

It is pleasing to me to be able to state that the present stock on hands is likely to meet a quick sale, and that the workmanship is highly creditable to the prisoners, and also to the officers who are in charge of the industrial department.

The present discipline is in no way interfered with in the carrying out of these labours, and I have much pleasure in stating that the general conduct of the prisoners has been good, and that their industrial employment serves materially to lessen the amount of irregularities which a too constant course of penal labour might bring about.

The general health of the prisoners has been good. There was only one death during the year, which was caused by a disease in the throat. There were no attempts made by prisoners to commit suicide, nor were any attempts made to escape.

I found the Medical Officer both attentive and punctual in the discharge of his duties, and the moral and religious instructions given by the respective clergymen to the prisoners under their charge have been constant and effectual in causing the good conduct which is to be noticed in the general amenable deportment of the prisoners.

All the prison buildings and fittings pertaining thereto have been kept in good repair by the officers of the Board of Public Works, and all requisitions on that department have been duly attended to.

I certify that the rules laid down for the government of the prison have been strictly complied with, except such particular cases as have been specially reported to, and brought under the notice of the Director.

I have the honour to be, sir,

Your most humble and obedient servant,

P. W. HACKETT, Governor.

To Captain Barlow,
Director of Irish Convict Prisons,
Dublin Castle.

CLASSIFIED STATEMENT of the NUMBER of OFFENCES committed by the Prisoners during the year ended 31st December, 1874.

Offences.	No.	Offences.	No.
Assault on convicts,	3	Injuring prison property,	6
Disobedience,	4	Other offences,	18
Disobedience and insolence,	4	Prohibited articles in possession,	3
Idleness,	1		
Insolence,	6	Total,	45

MOUNTJOY
MALE
CONVICT
PRISON.

*Governor's
Report.*

CLASSIFICATION of CRIMES for which those Prisoners have been sentenced who were received during the year ended 31st December, 1874.

Crimes.	No.	Crimes.	No.
Arson,	7	Manslaughter,	6
Assaulting,	1	Murder,	1
Assault to rob,	1	Malicious assault,	8
Assault and robbery,	3	Malicious assault on police,	1
Assault occasioning actual bodily		Malicious injury,	1
harm,	2	Military offences,	8
Bigamy,	2	Obtaining money—false pretences,	1
Burglary and felony,	9	Rape,	1
Burglary and robbery,	7	Receiving stolen goods,	5
Burglary, and former conviction,	1	Robbery with violence,	3
Burglary,	9	Robbery from person,	3
Breaking into shop and larceny,	1	Robbery,	2
Cattle stealing,	5	Sheep stealing, and former convic-	
Delivering threatening and menacing		tion,	3
messages,	1	Sheep stealing, and sacrilege,	1
Embezzlement,	2	Sheep stealing,	1
Felony, and former conviction,	1	Stealing from person, with vio-	
Feloniously stealing post letters,	2	lence,	1
Feloniously demanding meat and		Stealing hens, after previous con-	
bread,	1	viction for felony,	1
Felony,	2	Stealing hens and tackling, and	
Forging and uttering bill of exchange,	1	grievous assault on police,	1
Forgery,	2	Stealing clothes,	1
Highway robbery,	1	Stealing gun, and dangerous assault	
Horse-stealing,	3	with hatchet,	2
Housebreaking and robbery,	2	Wounding a mare,	1
Larceny and previous conviction,	22	Wounding,	1
Larceny from person,	13	Uttering base coin,	1
Larceny from dwelling,	1		
Larceny,	31	Total,	187

NUMBER of PRISONERS admitted in association during the year ended 31st December, 1874.

Trades.	No.	Trades.	No.
Shoemakers, from separation at		Removed Tailors,	1
Mountjoy Prison,	6	,, Shoemakers,	5
Manufacturers, from separation at		,, Manufacturers,	1
Mountjoy Prison,	1	,, Garden Labourers,	1
Remaining on 31st December, 1873,	35	,, Store Men,	1
		Remaining on 31st December, 1874,	35

RETURN of WORK performed in Manufacturing Departments during the year ended 31st December, 1874.

SHOEMAKING DEPARTMENT.		TAILORING DEPARTMENT.	
Making.		*Making.*	
Navvy Boots, pairs,	40	Ship mattress covers,	18
Blucher ,, ,,	186	Fend-off bags,	408
Warders' slippers, ,,	67	Calico Badges,	185
Matrons' ,, ,,	55	Slop trousers,	10
Men's Shoes, ,,	584	,, aprons,	2
Women's ,, ,,	210	Mattresses,	5
,, Boots, ,,	1	Chair Covers,	2
Frieze and Canvas slippers, pairs,	136		
Strait jackets,	6	*Repairing.*	
Horse collars,	2	Frock coats,	46
		Trousers,	53
Repairing.		Caps,	12
Strait jackets,	2	Vests,	12
Cots,	103	Top coats,	10
Boots,	28	Frieze jackets,	212
Slippers,	93	,, trousers,	807
Men's shoes,	368	,, vests,	153
Women's ,,	676		

RETURN of WORK performed in Manufacturing Departments—*con.*

TAILORING DEPARTMENT—*con.*

Frieze caps,	70
„ braces,	22
Hammocks,	83
Strait jackets,	4

MAT, MATTING, &c., DEPARTMENT.
Making.

Brush mats,	2,311
Chain „	1,101

MAT, MATTING, &c., DEPARTMENT—*con.*

Bordered mats,	1,809
Wool „	15
Wove „	141
Hearthrugs,	98
Coir scrubs,	7
Ship mattresses,	15
Matting, sq. yds.,	4,931
Fend-offs,	604

MOUNTJOY MALE CONVICT PRISON.

Governor's Report.

ESTIMATED VALUE of PRISONERS' WORK for the year ended 31st December, 1874.

Employment.	Daily average No. employed for 303 days.	Value of work performed.
		£ s. d.
Shoemaking,	22·26	254 9 3
Tailoring,	2·56	33 13 5
Mats, matting, &c., making,	44·05	471 16 4
Fend-off making,	2·74	62 8 6
Picking oakum,	52·7	85 6 3
Coopers and tinsmiths,	2·	75 15 0
Fatigue work, labourers, picking fibre, and net makers,	23·25	589 18 1
Non-effective,	5·9	—
Totals,	154·46	1,573 6 10

STATEMENT of the NUMBER of CONVICTS committed and disposed of, from 1st January to 31st December, 1874.

Received—

County and City Gaols,	155
Convict Depôts,	15
Military Barracks,	7
Licence forfeited cases,	10
Total,	187

Removed—

Convict Depôts,	189
Discharged,	11
Died,	1
Remaining in custody on 31st December, 1874,	135

TABLES showing the reported PREVIOUS IMPRISONMENT of the Prisoners received during the year ended 31st December, 1874.

Not reported to have been in prison before,	37	Eight times,	6	
Once,	34	Nine „	5	
Twice,	23	Ten „	3	
Three times,	19	Ten and under fifteen times,	5	
Four „	19	Fifteen times and over,	17	
Five „	6	Antecedents not known,	3	
Six „	8	Total,	187	
Seven „	2			

AGES of PRISONERS on CONVICTION, received during the year ended 31st December, 1874.

Fifteen and under twenty years of age,	21	Fifty and under sixty,	5
Twenty and under twenty-five,	45	Sixty and over,	7
Twenty-five and under thirty,	38		
Thirty and under forty,	48	Total,	187
Forty and under fifty,	23		

MOUNTJOY **SENTENCES** of the **PRISONERS** committed to this Prison during the year ended
MALE
CONVICT   31st December, 1874.
PRISON.

Five years' penal servitude,	-	- 107	Fourteen years' penal servitude,	-	2
Seven	„	„	- - 65	Life,	- - - - - - 1
Eight	„	„	- : 3		
Ten	„	„	- - 0	Total,	- - - 187

Governor's Report.

Single, 125.   Married, 62.

Roman Catholics, 140.   Protestants, 32.   Presbyterians, 6.

Jew, 1.   Unitarians, 1.

Medical Officer's Report.

MEDICAL OFFICER'S REPORT.

Mountjoy Male Prison,
January, 1875.

SIR,—I have the honour to lay before you my report of the sanitary condition of this prison for the past year, which I am happy to state has been most satisfactory.

The general health of the convicts has been very good, and I am glad to say that no outbreak of contagious or epidemic disease occurred in the prison during the year.

The dietary supplied to the prisoners has been wholesome and sound, and although it is not for the first four months of a very nutritions quality, as no meat is allowed, yet I believe that from its variety it is calculated to promote the health of the prisoners.

But one death occurred in the hospital, this was the result of acute laryngitis supervening on the chronic form.

Seven prisoners were removed to Spike Island Prison on medical grounds before they had completed their term in separation, 1 case of palpitation, 1 of dyspepsia inducing palpitation, 2 showing symptoms of mental disease from close confinement, 1 of general debility, 1 of consumption, and 1 of diseased thigh bone, who had suffered amputation of his right thigh before his reception here, and who was totally unfit for the discipline of this prison.

The admissions to hospital during the year were 54 as compared with 70 the year before, and the daily average number of sick in hospital was 4·03 as compared with 4·83 last year (1873). In addition to the above number, 10 prisoners were received into hospital from the Lusk establishment for treatment, but they are not included either in the admissions or in the daily average of sick in hospital, and their diseases will be found detailed in a separate table.

The health of the prison staff has been also very satisfactory, as there were only 6 warders who required treatment in hospital, 4 of whom were only detained for two or three days each from feverish colds, while the other two, 1 of cutaneous disease, and 1 of pleuro-pneumonia, were rather protracted.

The usual statistical returns will be found in the following tables.

I desire in conclusion to express my approval of the manner in which hospital warder Donohoe has discharged his duties during the year.

I have the honour to be, sir,

Your obedient servant,

J. W. YOUNG, M.D., Medical Officer.

To Captain Barlow,
the Director of Convict Prisons.

MOUNTJOY
MALE
CONVICT
PRISON.

*Medical
Officer's
Report.*

TABLE I.—HOSPITAL RETURN for the year 1874.

Number of prisoners in custody 1st January, 1874,   - 149
    „   „   received during the year,   - 187   336
    „   patients in hospital 1st January, 1874,   - 7
    „   „   admitted during the year,   - 54   61
    „   „   discharged from hospital.   - 48
    „   „   removed to Spike Island Prison,   - 7
    „   „   died in hospital,   - 1   61
    „   „   remaining in hospital, 1st January, 1875,   - 5

Daily average number of sick in hospital during the year,   - 4·03
Number of times prisoners were prescribed for in the prison, - 1,242
Daily average number prescribed for,   -   -   - 3·40

TABLE II.—PRISONERS removed to Spike Island Prison, from probation, on Medical grounds.

Date.	Register No.	Initials of Name.	Observations on case, as made in letter recommending Removal.
1874.			
Feb. 11,	8618	S. H., .	Palpitation, unfit for close confinement.
„ „	6615	W. H. S.,	Dyspepsia inducing palpitation.
„ 26,	8602	T. M‘K.,	Weakminded and unfit for cellular discipline.
June 30,	8704	J. F., .	General debility and loss of appetite.
„ „	8784	J. S., .	Consumption.
Sept. 29,	8814	H. D., .	Disease of bone, only one leg, unfit for this prison.
Oct. 14,	8805	T. D., .	Exhibits symptoms of mental disease.

TABLE III.—DEATHS during the Year.

Register No.	Initials of Name.	Received in Prison.	Admitted to hospital.	Date of Death.	Disease.
8266	J. D.,	10 Aug., 1871,	31 Mar., 1874,	18 April, 1874,	Laryngitis.

TABLE IV.—DISEASES of those admitted to HOSPITAL.

Scrofula,	- - -	3	Catarrh and Colds,	- 10	Rheumatism,	-	-	1
Sciatica,	- - -	1	Anthrax, -	- 1	Ophthalmia,	-	-	3
Syphilis,	- - -	5	Dropsy, -	- 1	Febrile affections,	-	-	1
Ulcers,	- - -	2	Whitlow,	- 1	Gum-boil, -	-	-	1
Gonorrhœa,	- -	2	Laryngitis,	- 1	Boils, -	-	-	1
Palpitation,	- -	1	Debility, -	- 1	Diarrhœa,	-	-	2
Nervous,	- -	1	Colic, -	- 1	Hœmorrhoids,	-	-	1
Observation,	-	10	Ear-ache, -	- 1	Bronchitis, -	-	-	1

TABLE V.—PRISONERS received from the LUSK ESTABLISHMENT for treatment in Hospital.

Register No.	Initials of Name.	Disease.	How disposed of.
8696	P. M., - -	Ulcer, - - -	Sent back to Lusk.
8709	J. H., - -	Ulcer, - - -	Do. do.
8733	M. M., - -	Tumour. - -	Discharged on licence.
8750	D. C., - -	Ulcer, - - -	Do. do.
8757	J. B., - -	Pneumonia, - -	Sent back to Lusk.
8758	M. M‘D., -	Bronchitis, -	Discharged on licence.
8820	J. B., - -	Gastric, - -	Sent back to Lusk.
8821	F. D., - -	Abscess, - -	Do. do.
8823	J. C., - -	Stricture, -	Do. do.
8847	J. B., - -	Bronchitis, -	Still in Hospital.

PROTESTANT CHAPLAIN'S REPORT.

Mountjoy Male Prison, Dublin,
January, 1875.

SIR,—During the past year the usual church services have been held, religious instructions given, and the convicts individually visited in their cells. I am happy to be able to say, as in former reports, that the conduct of the prisoners generally has been most satisfactory, their demeanour at Divine service reverent, their inquiries and answers at religious instruction intelligent, and their progress, under such circumstances, what might be expected.

During the course of the year I saw by the newspapers that a prisoner brought up for judgment, and about to be sentenced to a term of imprisonment, asked to be sentenced to penal servitude instead, a request that was granted. The inference drawn by writers in the public press from this circumstance was that penal servitude, after all, could not be a very severe punishment; and that criminals themselves preferred a sentence of five years' penal servitude to a term of imprisonment which could not exceed two years. Little do such writers know what penal servitude is in its stern reality, and less do they know of the sentiments and opinions of prisoners themselves on the subject. Immediately on reading the above circumstance and the comments made upon it, I questioned a man then under my charge here (he is so still) who upon his first conviction acted precisely in the same way, and was at that time also sentenced at his own request to penal servitude. Unhappily he is now a returned convict; but he told me that at his second trial, having then experience of what penal servitude really is, he would have been only too happy to have received the longest sentence of imprisonment that can be given rather than the shortest term of penal servitude. I may mention that this man soon after the expiration of the term (one year) to which he was about to be sentenced at his first trial, petitioned the Government to release him, making, as I am informed, the circumstance of his asking to be sentenced to penal servitude instead of imprisonment the ground of his application, and that his appeal was then successful. It may, however, be said, why are there many returned convicts when penal servitude is so severe and so dreaded by criminals?

Although reasons for such a state of things have often been put forward before, yet I would repeat a few of those which my experience of the criminal classes leads me to think will, to a great degree, at all events account for it.

1. Usually, I think, those who fall into crime are weaker than others to control themselves or to resist temptation.

2. Those who have fallen into crime and have been imprisoned, even if they have the very best desire to live honestly, often find it hard to obtain employment; employers will not give them work, often because the employed will not work with them.

3. Want of education, or worse still, ill education and bad training.

4. And though last not least, the terrible temptation of that nursery of crime and misery, the gigantic source of lamentation and mourning and woe—the public-house.

I am, sir, your faithful servant,

ROBERT FLEMYNG, A.M.,
Irish Church Chaplain.

To the Director of Government Prisons,
     Dublin Castle.

ROMAN CATHOLIC CHAPLAIN'S REPORT.

MOUNTJOY
MALE
CONVICT
PRISON.

Roman
Catholic
Chaplain's
Report.

Mountjoy Male Prison,
1st January, 1875.

SIR,—I have the honour to submit to you my report for the year 1874. The moral and religious conduct of the prisoners committed to my care has been regular and good, no punishments whatever having been recorded against any of them during the year for grave offences, and but few punishments for minor infractions of rule. The convicts have been on the whole well conducted at the religious instructions, which were given three or four times each week, as well as at the other religious exercises; and they seemed to profit by the advantages afforded them in the prison.

I have spent a considerable portion of my time in visiting the prisoners in their cells and workshops, and I have found them, with some rare exceptions, in good temper, quiet, orderly, and busily engaged in some practical, useful, or industrial work.

I think that the prison has been well managed during the year, and that the duties of the several officers, and in particular those of the masters placed over the discipline, the school, and the industrial training, have been performed with as much harmony as could be expected, and with considerable benefit to the convict service.

I have had pretty good opportunities of remarking the conduct of the officers in dealing with the prisoners, and I have to report that, as well as I could observe, the disciplinary rules, which are in themselves undoubtedly severe and stringent, have been enforced with a spirit of fairness, Christian kindness, and charity, which contributed very much to secure the ends aimed at in a reformatory prison, viz., the vindication of the law and the moral reformation of the criminal.

I ascribe, then, with great pleasure the good accomplished during the year to the care, the strict supervision, and exemplary conduct of the officers in charge of the several departments of the prison; and I believe that my ministrations would have been in a great measure inoperative, if not in many instances utterly fruitless, without their co-operation.

In fact, sir, every year's experience tends to confirm me in the belief that the effect of prison discipline and of prison management mainly depends upon the character and spirit of the officers administering it. If all the officers, and especially the superior officers, are really honest men, prudent and kindhearted, and at the same time firm and resolute when the occasion demands it, never harsh and hard towards the men under them, the discipline and management of the prison will be effective in repressing crime and conducive to the moral amendment of the criminal.

I have the honour to be, sir,

Your most obedient servant,

MICHAEL CODY,
Roman Catholic Chaplain.

Captain Barlow,
Director of Convict Prisons, Dublin Castle.

PRESBYTERIAN CHAPLAIN'S REPORT.

The Manse, 49 Great Charles-street, Dublin,
1st January, 1875.

Sir,—My official statement for 1874 may be presented in few words.

I have to report that the number of prisoners in attendance on my ministration has been somewhat less than in former years, that Divine service on Sabbath, and the weekly visitation from cell to cell, have been regularly performed, either personally, or, in my absence from the city by a competent substitute, that the demeanour of the prisoners has been uniformly attentive and decorous, and that the conduct of all the officers with whom I have come in contact has been, as heretofore, courteous and helpful.

I have the honour to remain, sir,

Your obedient servant,

Robert Hanna, Presbyterian Chaplain.

The Director of Government Prisons,
Dublin Castle.

HEAD SCHOOLMASTER'S REPORT.

Mountjoy Male Prison,
11th January, 1875.

Sir,—I beg leave to submit to you my report of Mountjoy Male Prison School, for the year ended the 31st of December, 1874, which is my twentieth annual report in the Convict Service.

Reading, writing, and the four simple rules of arithmetic, are the course of instruction in the school, in pursuance of Director's memo. of the 16th of November, 1869.

The prisoners are divided into two prison classes—probation and association. The probation prisoners, about four-fifths of the whole, attend school by day, and the association prisoners, one-fifth of the whole, attend school in the evening after the labours of the day. The longest time allowed to any prisoner at school is an hour per day, and that only to those learning First and Second Books. Those learning higher Books—Third and Fourth, are allowed only three attendances weekly for an hour each time. The association class attend school for an hour every evening, except Saturday evening.

In eight months (the probationer's time here) for an hour or half an hour daily at school the progress cannot be very marked, of aged uncultivated minds long vitiated with other than self-improving thoughts; the task of preparing many of them to pay any attention to education is not an easy one.

At the end of the year 1873 there were on school-rolls, . . . 146
Admitted to school during the year 1874, ... 165
Transferred from school to other prisons, &c., in 1874, . . 187
Remaining on rolls and account books 31st December, 1874, . 124

Of 165 admitted 38 were wholly illiterate (First Book).
"   "   49 were nearly so (Second Book).

Thus showing that more than one-half of the Convicts admitted to school during the year were unable to read or write at reception; also showing that the classes in society to which the Convicts belong, and

from which they have been taken, are annually becoming more intelligent, and their moral tone improving; as two-thirds of last year's
admissions to school were wholly illiterate or nearly so, as stated in my
last report. The illiterate ones of '73 were inferior in conduct to the
illiterates of this past year, 1874.

In reading alone there have been 80 promotions during the year, as
follows:—

From First or lowest Book to Second Book, ... 18
From Second Book to Third Book, ... 25
From Third Book to Fourth Book, ... 37
                                                            80

Of 187 transferred from school to other Prisons, &c.,—
  60 could write well.
  83 well enough for ordinary business.
  43 could write, but not well.
   1 could not write any.

77 per cent. of the whole could write fairly.

38 of these worked proportion and practice in arithmetic.
16 „   worked compound rules.
108 „   worked the simple rules.
25 „   could only make figures and knew some notation.
  ———
187

86 per cent. of the whole worked simple rules and above them.

Remaining at school on rolls and books, 31st December, 1874, . 124.
  Reading First or lowest Book, . . . 18
    „   Second or next Book, . . . 34
    „   Third Book. 34
    „   Fourth Book, ... 38
                      Total, . . 124

48 of these could write small hand well.
58 „   „   write fairly.
18 „   „   write large hand.
———
124

30 work proportion and above in arithmetic.
20 „   compound rules.
65 „   simple rules.
 9 making figures and rudiments of notation.

As the services of the Assistant Schoolmaster were dispensed with on
the 1st of last April, I must be very active to keep all the classes
taught during their *short school time*, which I am enabled to do by the
assistance of the warder in charge, who is selected for his suitableness by
the "Local Authorities," who pay much attention to the school. I must
here express my acknowledgment of the valuable aid afforded me in *turn*
by warders M'Manus, Hicks, and Gaynor.

In order that my whole time may be devoted to teaching during
school time, I endeavoured to discharge all the other duties connected
with the school before and after school hours. These duties are various,
viz.—filling up school accounts, giving out and receiving school books,
preparing class sheets on removal of prisoners, examining and classifying
prisoners on reception, dealing out books to them, &c.

The school for the probation class begins at 11 o'clock, and the average
attendance for the first hour, from 11 to 12 o'clock, is about 30; but
these being learning First and Second Books are divided into many

MOUNTJOY
MALE
CONVICT
PRISON.
—
*Head
School-
master's
Report.*

sections, and require much instruction in order to improve and forward them.

The best section of the Second Book class, and the Third and Fourth Book classes, attend school from 12 to 1 o'clock, and number about 30 at each attendance every alternate day. They are all taught by myself except whilst writing, which the warder in charge superintends. From 6 to 7 o'clock the associated class attend school.

The conduct at school has been very good, and a very strong desire for improvement has prevailed during the year, with a few exceptions.

I have the honour to be, sir,

Your most obedient servant,

MICHAEL HAROLD, Head Schoolmaster.

To Captain J. Barlow,
The Director of Irish Government Prisons,
Dublin Castle.

SPIKE ISLAND CONVICT PRISON.

SPIKE
ISLAND
PRISON.
—
*Director's
Report.*

With the exception of the abolition of the office of Inspector, to which I have already alluded, and the appointment of a Deputy Governor, no change has taken place in the Prison arrangements; the Governor's clerk, Mr. G. Sheehan, has been appointed Deputy Governor and still performs some of the office duties. I believe the change will be of service to the Prison. I visit the Prison monthly, this to a great extent renders the constant attendance of an officer with superior powers to those of the Governor unnecessary, whilst the presence on the island at all times of a Deputy Governor with full powers to act during the absence of the Governor cannot fail to be advantageous to the discipline of the Prison; the arrangements, however, throw additional correspondence upon both the Governor and myself. The Prison has, as I have had occasion for some years to expect, been worked in a most satisfactory, and as far as its exceptional circumstances will admit of, an economical manner. The general conduct of the subordinate officers has been good; some dismissals and discharges, unavoidable in a large staff, took place. I trust that the improved scale of pay sanctioned to the subordinate officers may prevent the inconvenience which arise from constant changes in the staff.

The general health of the staff has been good; I regret to have to report, however, the death of two warders during the year.

The general health of the convicts has been good; a marked increase in the number of externs attending the hospital appears, but this is I believe the result of entering cases which were not formerly noted.

The employments have been the same as in former years, with this exception, that for a portion of the year the entire labour of the convicts was not required by the Naval Department at Haulbowline, the labour thus available was utilised by the Royal Engineer Department at Spike Island.

The Governor's report as to the mode in which repairs, &c., are
carried out by the Royal Engineer have been alluded to by me
in a former report.

The general conduct of the convicts has been good, three at-
tempted to escape but did not succeed in doing so; in six cases
it was necessary, owing to dangerous assaults and other grave
misconduct, to order corporal punishments. I quite concur with
the Governor's remarks as to the change for the worse which has
taken place in the class of convicts we now receive, the great
majority being of the habitual criminal class; sixteen or seventeen
years ago a large proportion was countrymen who had been
driven into crime during the famine year and those succeeding
it; these men were not alone far more manageable in prison, but
gave reasonable ground for believing that on release they would
not return to criminal courses.

During the year some convicts were removed to Dundrum
Criminal Lunatic Asylum. The weak minded, imbecile, and eccentric prisoners, who although they cannot be certified as insane,
are undoubtedly to a certain extent irresponsible, have as usual
been a source of trouble to the authorities. It will I believe become
absolutely necessary to make some special arrangements for them
eventually. Some years past I suggested that provision might
be made for their proper care by building a small prison at Lusk,
by convict labour, by treating them at Mountjoy Male Prison, or
by erecting a special building for them at Spike Island. Should
any change in the Irish Prison arrangements be contemplated
probably some more satisfactory and economical arrangement may
be made.

The usual Reports with Statistics from the Governor, Chaplains,
Medical Officer, and Head Schoolmaster, are appended.

J. BARLOW, *Director.*

GOVERNOR'S REPORT.

Spike Island Government Prison,
January, 1875.

SIR,—In accordance with your directions I have the honour to submit
my report for the year 1874, which is the twentieth annual report I have
made as Governor of Spike Island Convict Depôt.

First,—The Honorable R. Netterville, who had been for many years
in the service—first as Governor of Mountjoy Prison, and then as
Inspector here—retired from the service in September. The office of
Inspector being abolished, and a Deputy Governor appointed in lieu, Mr.
G. Sheehan, first clerk, and a very efficient and experienced officer, getting
the post.

The subordinate staff had been unsettled for some time, and a good
many vacancies existed, owing partly to the question of salary, and partly
to the difficulty of candidates passing the Civil Service examination. The
salary question has now been remedied by the increase which took effect
in April, but several vacancies still exist. Twenty-three new appointments were made during the year. Seven were dismissed the service
for breaches of discipline and other irregularities of conduct, two died,
eight resigned, and seven were discharged as unfit for the service on

medical and other grounds. It is to be hoped that with the increased pay
the staff will, in future, be more settled and permanent, as changes and
want of experience on the part of discipline officers are very great dis-
advantages in the working of a public works prison.

I am able to speak with satisfaction of the general good conduct,
attention, and discipline of the great majority of the subordinate officers,
and the Chief Warder and Principal Warders have been as usual—steady,
zealous, and efficient in the discharge of their duties.

A return in the statistics herewith forwarded will show the number of
prisoners in custody on the 1st January, 1874, the number received
during the year, and their disposal. The respective sentences have been
carried out strictly in the manner prescribed by the rules, and, as usual,
every prisoner had the opportunity daily afforded him of speaking to me
on any matter affecting himself, his position, or treatment.

By far the larger proportion of the prisoners were employed the same
as of late years on the docks in progress of being made at Haulbowline;
a block of new offices were also built there by convict labour, and the
several trades carried on as usual, viz., stone-cutting, shoemaking, mason,
smith, and carpenter work.

About seventy of those usually on the dock work were employed at
Spike Island, in building blocks of cottages for warders' quarters, truck-
ing materials to same, and quarrying and stone-breaking, but several of
those at the latter employments were of the weak-minded and invalid
classes, and consequently unfit for any other out-door labour.

Daily average number on the works (prison works included),   632
Not employed (in cells and hospital), ...   32

Total, ...   664

The working hours were the same as in former years.

The buildings are in fair order and repair, but some of the roofs are
beginning to get leaky, and will soon require to be renewed. The Royal
Engineer Department are responsible for all necessary repairs, and the
alterations found to be necessary from time to time are, as a rule, also
carried out under their superintendence, and subject to their approval;
but the system is by no means satisfactory, and does not work well, the
prison authorities having no control or check either over the work, the
time at which it is done, or the expenditure incurred in the execution of
it. In my annual report for the year 1863, and again in my last annual
report, I ventured respectfully to submit the great advantage, as well as
the annual saving to be effected by having an experienced and competent
officer on the staff in the position of clerk of works, who would superin-
tend and direct all works in progress by convict labour, but especially
new buildings, alterations, and repairs; an officer of this rank is, I believe,
attached to each of the English convict prisons.

Three convicts made unsuccessful attempts at escapes, two from off the
works outside the prison, and one to break out by night. Six received
corporal punishment for assaults on warders, idling on the works, and
other insubordinate conduct. In the month of April a convict committed
suicide by strangling himself in his cell. He was eccentric, and the
coroner's jury returned a verdict of "suicide whilst labouring under
temporary insanity," and added that there was no neglect on the part of
the officials. Seven convicts were sent to Dundrum Lunatic Asylum,
having been certified insane, but in one case only, that of a fever patient,
did the insanity appear to originate here. The conduct of the prisoners
generally has been good, and, with a larger daily average of prisoners
than in the previous year, the total number of offences against the rules

were less by 138; but, as will always be the case, there are a few individual prisoners who are insubordinate in their conduct generally. In no case, however, was there any combination for misconduct, or for opposition in connexion with the work; but I would here take the opportunity of stating, as the result of my experience, that the convict class of the present day are chiefly what I might call "professionals" in their calling, the great majority being of the "habitual criminal" class of the large towns, and military offenders, who have been convicted or turned out of the army, and they are by no means so manageable or amenable either to discipline or labour as the convicts of fifteen or twenty years ago, who were then more of the agricultural class, and very different in conduct, character, and demeanour. *Governor's Report.*

The Sunday and week-day services have been regularly attended to and carried on by the chaplains of the respective persuasions, and school held every week-day evening after the day's work was over.

I have not seen, or received intimation of, any abuse or abuses not reported by me.

The usual statistical returns for the year are forwarded herewith.

I hereby certify that the rules laid down for the government of the prison have been complied with during the past year, except in such cases as have been reported to, or brought under the notice of, the Director.

I have the honour to be, sir, your most obedient servant,

P. HAY, Governor.

Captain Barlow, &c., &c., &c.,
    Director of Government Prisons,
        Dublin Castle.

RETURN showing the CRIMES of 682 CONVICTS in CUSTODY 31st December, 1874.

Murder,	16
Shooting at with intent to murder,	13
Attempting to kill and murder one Owen M'Fadden,	1
Being one of an armed party who fired on a party of the Royal Irish Constabulary,	1
Manslaughter,	32
Stabbing, cutting, and wounding,	5
Felonious, grievous, malicious, and other assaults,	21
Assault and robbery,	11
Assault with intent to rob,	1
Found armed at night with a dangerous and offensive weapon with intent then to break and enter into a dwelling-house and commit felony therein,	1
Demanding money and other articles with menaces and by force,	2
Assaulting dwelling-house,	2
Compelling to quit dwelling-house,	3
Unlawful assembly, breaking into habitation, and carrying away arms,	2
Arson and attempt at arson,	17
Highway robbery,	11
Whiteboy offence,	1
Burglary and robbery,	44
Burglary and previous conviction,	23
Robbery,	10
Housebreaking and robbery,	41
Felony and previous conviction,	15
Felony of Post letters,	5
Writing and sending threatening letters,	4
Rape, and aiding,	17
Perjury,	2
Forgery,	5
Embezzlement,	2
Uttering forged Post Office Order for money,	1
Fradulently removing from documents stamps with intent that use should be made of them,	1
Stealing from the person,	70
Larceny and previous conviction,	210
Cattle stealing,	14
Horse stealing,	10
Sheep stealing,	14
Sacrilege,	2
Receiving stolen goods,	14
Receiving goods and money by means of false pretences,	6
Having base coin in possession,	4
Carnal knowledge of females under ten years,	2
Indecent assault on male persons,	2
Buggery,	1
Attempt to commit buggery,	2
By fraud and force detaining a female child under fourteen years of age,	1
Bigamy,	2
Malicious injury to machinery,	3
Military offences,	16
Total,	**682**

SPIKE
ISLAND
PRISON.

Governor's
Report.

RETURN showing the NUMBER of CONVICTS in CUSTODY, committed and disposed of during the Year ended 31st December, 1874.

COMMITTED.		HOW DISPOSED OF.	
1st January, 1874—		31st December, 1874—	
In custody, - -	650	Remaining in custody, - -	682
Committed from—		Removed during the year to—	
Mountjoy Prison, - -	181	Mountjoy for Lusk, - -	56
		Cork County Gaol, - -	1
		Dundrum Lunatic Asylum, -	7
		Released on licence, - -	39
		Discharged on completion of sentence, - - -	36
		Discharged on commutation of sentence, - - -	1
		Committed suicide, - -	1
		Died, - - - -	6
Total, - -	831	Total, - -	831

RETURN showing the SENTENCES and the AGES on CONVICTION of 682 CONVICTS in CUSTODY, 31st December, 1874.

SENTENCES.		SENTENCES.	
Five Years' Penal Servitude, -	220	Life penal servitude, - -	35
Six „ „ -	1	Life transportation, - -	6
Seven „ „ -	299		
Eight „ „ -	2		
Ten „ „ -	75		
Fourteen „ „ -	23		
Fifteen „ „ -	8		
Twenty „ „ -	12		
Twenty-five „ „ -	1		
	641		41

Total, 682.

AGES ON CONVICTION.

Under Twenty Years, - - - - -	62
Twenty and under Twenty-five, - - - -	142
Twenty-five and under Thirty, - - - -	146
Thirty and under Thirty-five, - - - -	118
Thirty-five and under Forty, - - - -	67
Forty and under Fifty, - - - - -	91
Fifty and under Sixty, - - - - -	27
Sixty and under Seventy, - - - -	7
Seventy and under Eighty, - - - -	1
Eighty and under Ninety, - - - -	1
Total, - - - - -	682

ABSTRACT ACCOUNT showing the ESTIMATED VALUE of the PRODUCTIVE LABOUR of the Prisoners, and the NUMBER EMPLOYED during the Year ended 31st December, 1874.

How Employed.	Daily Average Number Employed for 303 days.	Estimated Value of Work performed.		Total.	
		£ s. d.		£ s. d.	
PRISON WORKS.					
Tailors, - - - -	11	416 12 6			
Shoemakers, - - - -	6	227 5 0			
Carpenters and Sawyers, - -	5	189 7 6			
Do. beginners.	4	90 18 0			
Smiths and Nailers, - -	1	45 9 0			
Do. beginners, -	1	30 6 0			
Painters, - - - -	2	75 15 0			
Masons, - - - -	8	363 12 0			
Bakers, - - - -	5	227 5 0			
Tinsmiths and Coopers, - -	2	60 12 0			
Repairing Beds, Socks, &c., -	7	106 1 0			
Labourers in Prison Garden and on Prison Works generally, -	89	1,346 7 0			
Washing in Laundry, - -	10	303 0 0			
Cooks, - - - -	5	75 15 0			
Fatigue work, Cleaning, and Messing,	24	363 12 0			
Boatmen, - - - -	6	90 18 0			
Oakum Picking (on wet days), -	6	22 14 6			
Do. (Invalids), -	22	27 15 6			
	214			4,065 5 0	
ROYAL ENGINEER WORKS.					
Labourers, - - -	35	530 5 0			
	35			530 5 0	
WAR DEPARTMENT (HAULBOWLINE).					
Labourers, - - -	9	204 10 6			
	9			204 10 6	
ADMIRALTY WORKS (HAULBOWLINE).					
Stonecutters and Masons, -	37	1,494 16 0			
Do. beginners,	24	484 16 0			
Carpenters and Sawyers, -	13	525 4 0			
Do. beginners,	6	136 7 0			
Smiths and Nailers, - -	4	161 12 0			
Do. beginners,	6	136 7 0			
Shoemakers, - - -	4	151 10 0			
Do. beginners, -	2	45 9 0			
Labourers, Quarrymen, &c., -	277	5,595 8 0			
Oakum Picking (on wet days), -	1	3 15 9			
	374			8,735 4 9	
Total, - - -	632			13,535 5 3	

Daily average number employed, - - - - 632
   ,,   ,,   not employed (in cells and hospital), - 32

Total daily average, - - - 664

MEDICAL OFFICER'S REPORT.

Spike Island Convict Prison,
11th January, 1875.

SIR,—I have the honour to submit the annual report on the state of health of the officers and the prisoners, as well as on the general sanitary condition of this prison, and the usual medical statistics for the year 1874.

There were 52 of the subordinate officers treated in hospital and in

SPIKE
ISLAND
PRISON.

*Medical
Officer's
Report.*

quarters during the year, two of whom died, and four were discharged the service on medical grounds.

Of the 181 prisoners received here during the year, 25 were found to be suffering from some disease or delicacy rendering them unfit for ordinary prison labour. These received special attention, and were placed at such employment as best suited the particular circumstances of their individual cases.

During the year there were 230 prisoners treated in hospital for ailments generally of a light and varied character, chiefly—simple fever, bronchitis, diarrhœa, wounds and contusions, colic, abscesses, inflammation of the tonsils, and rheumatism—diseases such as might be expected, and are usually found, amongst labourers employed at out-door work.

Seven deaths occurred during the year among the convicts, six of the number being persons of advanced age, labouring under some organic disease or general delicacy of long standing, and one, I regret having to report, was from suicide. This prisoner was placed in separation for some breach of prison rules. Soon after the charge was investigated, and before the decision was communicated to him he suspended himself by placing a cord, made of oakum (which was given to him to pick), around his neck, one end being attached to the bell-handle of his cell. When discovered he was dead. The full particulars of the case were officially reported at the time of the lamentable occurrence.

During the year seven prisoners who were found to be insane were transferred to the Central Criminal Lunatic Asylum, Dundrum. There are still in this establishment a number of weak-minded and eccentric convicts, who are unfit for the ordinary prison discipline, and require exceptional treatment. These are exceedingly difficult to manage while in association with the other prisoners, and I take this opportunity again respectfully to urge the necessity of providing a separate building for their special treatment.

It is most gratifying to observe that during the year no epidemic or infectious disease appeared among the convicts, and that no permanent sanitary defect presented itself. The deficiency of rain during the summer caused some anxiety as to the supply of water, but judicious arrangements and care averted any scarcity being felt in this respect.

The Governor and the other officers of this prison have invariably rendered me effective support. The resident apothecary has performed his duties with zeal and efficiency.

I have the honour to be, sir,

Your most obedient servant,

P. O'KEEFFE, M.D., Medical Officer.

Captain Barlow,
    Director of Convict Prisons,
        Dublin Castle.

---

*Medical
Statistics.*

MEDICAL STATISTICS for the Year 1874.

Number of sick in hospital on the 1st January, 1874,	12
„ admitted during the year,	230
Total,	**242**
Of these were discharged from hospital,	221
Died during the year,	7
Remaining in hospital on 1st January, 1875,	14
Total,	**242**

Daily average number of sick treated in hospital during the year, - 14·89　SPIKE
Number of Warders treated in hospital during the year, - - 46　ISLAND
Number of Warders who died during the year, - - 2　PRISON.
Number of externs treated during the year, - - 22,093　————
Daily average number of externs treated during the year, - - 60·526 *Medical Statistics.*

Number of DISEASES treated in Hospital during the Year.

Bronchitis, -	34	Ear-ache, -	6
Phthisis, -	3	Ophthalmia, -	4
Pneumonia, -	3	Colica, -	10
Pleuritis, -	3	Erysipelas, -	1
Asthma, -	3	Stricture of urethra, -	2
Hæmoptysis, -	3	Abscess, -	9
Melena, -	1	Heart Disease, -	7
Simple continued Fever, -	39	Paralysis of bladder, -	1
Diarrhœa, -	21	Rheumatism, -	6
Syncope, -	2	Tonsillitis, -	9
Debility, -	7	Epistaxis, -	1
Constipation, -	4	Orchitis, -	1
Dyspepsia, -	3	Boils, -	1
Anorexia, -	2	Dropsy, -	2
Wounds, contusions, &c., -	19	Gastritis, -	2
Anasarca, -	2	Cephalalgia, -	1
Epilepsy, -	7	Fracture of femur, -	1
Observation, -	5	Ulcers, -	3
Scald, -	1		
Hip disease, -	1	Total, -	230

MORTALITY TABLE.

Register Number.	Initials of Name.	Date of Admission into Hospital.	Date of Death.	Cause of Death.
13,132	P. P.	30th March, 1874.	4th April, 1874.	Fever and bronchitis.
13,925	J. D.	Occurred in separate cells.	6th　,,　,,	Suicide.
13,279	H. M'G.	13th April, 1874.	14th　,,　,,	Choleraic diarrhœa.
11,538	M. C.	14th　,,　,,	25th May, ,,	Paralysis of bladder.
14,045	C. M'C.	26th Sept., ,,	18th Dec., ,,	Cancer of stomach.
13,537	P. W.	19th Dec., ,,	23rd　,,　,,	Acute bronchitis.
13,934	J. W.	27th Oct., ,,	23th　,,　,,	Dropsy.

The following is a LIST of INSANE PRISONERS transferred to DUNDRUM CRIMINAL LUNATIC ASYLUM during the Year.

Register No.	Initials of Name.	Where convicted.	Date of conviction.	Received into Prison.	Sent to Asylum.
14,071	J. E.	Dublin, -	14 Oct., 1873,	25 July, 1874,	15 Oct., 1874,
12,727	P. M.	Cork, -	16 Mar., 1865,	23 Feb., 1866,	21　,,　,,
12,628	J. B.	Clonmel,	20 July, 1866,	21 Sept., 1866,	,,　,,　,,
13,281	J. K.	Dublin, -	26 Oct., 1868,	8 July, 1869,	,,　,,　,,
13,758	M. L.	Dublin, -	9 Feb., 1870,	21 Mar., 1870,	14 Dec., ,,
13,759	W. S.	Nenagh, -	8 Mar., 1871,	7 June, 1871,	,,　,,　,,
13,703	W. M.	Nenagh, -	28 June, 1871,	21 Mar., 1872,	30　,,　,,

SPIKE
ISLAND
PRISON.

*Protestant
Chaplain's
Report.*

PROTESTANT CHAPLAIN'S REPORT.

Spike Island Government Prison,
January 12th, 1875.

SIR,—I have the honour to present my report for the year ending 31st December, 1874. During that period Divine service was performed on 54 occasions, Lord's Supper administered four times, prisoners catechised 48 times, hospital and cells 118 times.

Throughout the year the prisoners under my charge behaved themselves remarkably well, and were always attentive and well conducted on both Sundays and lecture days. There was no instance of insubordination save one, in the case of a prisoner who was rather troublesome, to refer to, and beg to state that everything has been carried out by me in accordance with the rules during the period referred to.

I have the honour to be, sir,

Your obedient servant,

JOSEPH G. BOUCHIER, Protestant Chaplain.

To Captain Barlow,
   Director Government Prisons,
      Castle, Dublin.

ROMAN CATHOLIC CHAPLAIN'S REPORT.

Spike Island, 1st January, 1875.

SIR,—In forwarding to you my report for the year 1874, I beg to state that the several duties prescribed for the Roman Catholic Chaplains were duly discharged during the year. The Roman Catholic prisoners were assembled every morning, on week days, in the prison chapel for morning prayer, and twice on each Sunday and holiday for Divine service and sermons. A large number of them attended also every Saturday, and on several holidays, for catechetical instructions and confession, preparatory to the reception of the sacraments, and I feel enabled to state that the majority of them received the sacraments of penance and the Holy Eucharist at least once during the year; some of them did so weekly or monthly. To attain this happy result I endeavoured by Divine grace, first, to make them fully understand the doctrines and practices of their Holy Faith, and then to impress upon their minds the great truths of religion, such as the greatness and goodness of God, the enormity of sin, the happiness of the elect, and the fear of death, judgment, and hell. It was not until they appeared truly repentant of their past misdeeds, and firmly resolved on amendment of life, proved in their exterior conduct, that they were admitted to the Holy Communion.

I daily visited the sick in hospital, and oftener when necessary, and administered to them all the necessary services and consolations of religion. This I always consider to be a most essential duty, as there is no duty of more vital importance than to prepare the dying Christian for a holy and happy death.

In compliance with the prison rule, I daily read and initialed the letters written by the prisoners to their friends before posting, and also the letters coming into the prison for them, and delivered individually such as were unobjectionable. This duty occupied a good deal of time, however, I consider the rule a very wise and salutary one.

I visited the prisoners confined in the punishment cells once or twice a day, and administered to them such counsel and admonitions as their offences appeared to me to require ; and I may add that I have lost no opportunity by my counsel and influence to co-operate with the prison authorities in carrying out the discipline of the prison, and in promoting the peace, order, and general welfare of the officers and prisoners.

Spike Island Prison.

Roman Catholic Chaplain's Report.

I have the honour to be, sir,

Your very obedient servant,

T. F. LYONS, R. C. Chaplain.

Captain Barlow, Director, &c.

ASSISTANT ROMAN CATHOLIC CHAPLAIN'S REPORT.

Assistant Roman Catholic Chaplain's Report.

Spike Island Prison,
12th January, 1875.

SIR,—I beg to lay before you my report for the past year. It affords me pleasure to be able to say that the conduct of the prisoners under my charge has been, generally speaking, good. It is no wonder that amongst so large a number, some of whom have led irregular lives, there should be found a few who did not give satisfaction, and who committed breaches of discipline, but the vast majority of them conducted themselves well, and seemed to take an interest in performing the work allotted to them ; this I can bear testimony to, as I have often seen them at their work during the year.

I have attended as usual in the mornings and given out morning prayer and meditation, and visited the prison a second time in the course of the day to see the prisoners confined in cells for violating prison rules, on whom I have expended much time in reproving, correcting, and advising them. Religious instructions have been given every Sunday and holiday during the entire year, the hospitals visited daily and sometimes oftener, according as necessity required it. Opportunities were given to the prisoners every Saturday of frequenting the sacraments, and complying with their religious duties. I would wish to be able to say that all availed themselves of these opportunities. There were, however, some exceptions. I shall endeavour to induce these to do as the rest have done.

I have the honour to be, sir,

Your obedient servant,

JOHN MURPHY,
Assistant Roman Catholic Chaplain.

Captain Barlow, Director.

PRESBYTERIAN CHAPLAIN'S REPORT.

Presbyterian Chaplain's Report.

Spike Island, 11th January, 1875.

SIR,—I beg leave to lay before you my report for the year 1874.

In the regular discharge of my duties the year has passed over without any marked distinguishing feature. I can testify for the prisoners committed to my charge that they are attentive and serious while I teach them from the Scriptures, and that they take kindly what I say to them personally. It would give me pleasure if I could this year speak of any evident good results among those whose term of imprisonment has closed,

SPIKE
ISLAND
PRISON.

Presby-
terian
Chaplain's
Report.

as I have been able to do in some former years. But for the present I can only hope.

Whatever those who have not been engaged in such duties as mine may be led to imagine, those who have experience in them know that the hope of reform in individuals reared and entangled among the criminal classes can never be great, and that in this department of the work we must be thankful for very small mercies. There are others coming from rural employments or from the army who have fallen under the just sentence of the law in consequence of one offence, some of whom while enduring their sentence have the cynosure of a wife and little ones at home to whom they turn their eyes, while they wait for the day of liberation from their house of servitude, and their return to the home and happiness they have forfeited. Whatever real hope there is of reform among convicts has its subjects principally in this class. If they can be saved from the very evil influences among which their crimes have brought them, their period of punishment may be blessed to teach them lessons which they failed to learn, and probably never would have learned in happier circumstances. In saying this I am speaking of what I have known to take place in more than one or two instances.

I have regularly visited the prisoners who were in hospital, and also those confined in the punishment cells.

I have the honour to be, sir,

Your very obedient servant,

W. J. KERTLAND, LL.D.,
Presbyterian Chaplain.

Captain Barlow,
Director of Convict Prisons,
Dublin Castle.

HEAD SCHOOLMASTER'S REPORT.

Head
School-
master's
Report.

Spike Island Convict Prison,
January 20, 1875.

Sir,—In compliance with your directions, I have the honour to submit my annual report for 1874.

At the close of the past year the number on the school roll in the first or lowest class was 27 ; in the second, 73 ; in the third, 142 ; and in the exempt class, attending of their own accord, 57, making a total of 299 prisoners.

All the classes, as usual, write on paper. The prisoners able to read and write sufficiently well for all practical purposes, with people in their station of life, are exempt from school attendance. But a considerable number of this class are found very desirous to continue at school. The privilege of so doing is extended to as many as the schoolroom can accommodate without overcrowding. Applicants have therefore to wait for vacancies to occur before they can be admitted. The permission to attend accorded to prisoners in the exempt class is conditional, to continue while the numbers in the ordinary classes remain low enough to afford the needful accommodation, and so long as their conduct at school is perfectly satisfactory.

Any prisoner advanced in years who is found to have no mind to learn, and also any prisoner discovered to be excessively dull and inapt to learn, are exempted from further attendance. The prompt elimination of such prisoners has had a very beneficial effect.

Spike
Island
Prison.

Head
School-
master's
Report.

The subjects taught include arithmetic, as well as reading, spelling, and writing, besides such general information as may be imparted by the reading of the very instructive school books, and the elucidation of the subject-matter of the lessons.

The prisoners in general, I am happy to report, are making fair progress. Their conduct under instructions is, as a rule, very satisfactory. With hardly an exception, they manifest a desire to learn, and endeavour to profit as much as possible by the opportunities here afforded them.

The library is availed of very fully by the prisoners able to read. An addition of nearly 100 volumes has been made to it. The new books are the best selection of the approved works already on the catalogue, and are thoroughly well bound, a matter of no small importance in a prison library. The prisoners appear to appreciate the new books very much, and seem well pleased to find several copies of a popular work, instead of but one, as heretofore.

In conclusion, I feel bound in justice to my colleague, Mr. Ryan, to testify that he discharges his difficult, and sometimes very critical, duties with his usual zeal and ability.

I have the honour to be, sir,

Your most obedient servant,

EDWARD M'GAURAN, Head Schoolmaster.

Captain Barlow, &c., &c., &c.,
Director of Convict Prisons.

MOUNTJOY FEMALE CONVICT PRISON.

Mountjoy
Female
Convict
Prison.

Director's
Report.

No material change has taken place during the past year in the arrangements of this prison.

I regret I cannot report favourably as to the conduct of the discipline officers of this prison; but, as I have before remarked, there are doubtless exceptions, some changes already made in the prison staff, and some which I trust to have sanctioned during the present year will, I believe, prevent any such misconduct as took place in the past year.

The employments of the convicts remain unchanged during the present year. I hope to obtain the washing of a large Government department. If this is undertaken at the female prison, suitable employment will be provided for a portion of the convicts, whilst some saving to the public will result. It will also enable the prisoners to become fair laundresses. The ordinary prison washing does not enable the laundry matrons to teach them as fully as is desirable to do it, in order to enable them to earn their livelihood on discharge.

Some changes in the staff have taken place during the past year. The resignation of the Roman Catholic chaplain, the Rev. Dr. Buckcridge, caused a vacancy, which was filled up by the promotion of the Assistant Roman Catholic chaplain, Rev. B. Fitzpatrick, the Rev. M. Walsh being appointed Resident Chaplain in his stead.

MOUNTJOY
FEMALE
CONVICT
PRISON.

*Director's
Report.*

The conduct of the prisoners was, with the exception of the misconduct I have referred to in the opening portion of my report, much the same as in previous years; the disturbance to which I allude was owing to the dislike shown by a portion of the prisoners to an officer who did her duty fearlessly and conscientiously. The prisoners are now in a proper state of discipline. I do not anticipate any further serious misconduct. The health of the convicts has been generally good.

I attach the usual reports from superintendent medical officers, chaplains, and head schoolmistresses, together with the usual statistics.

J. BARLOW.

*Superinten-
dent's
Report.*

SUPERINTENDENT'S REPORT.

Mountjoy Female Prison,
31st March, 1875.

SIR,—I have the honour to forward to you my annual report for the year ending the 31st December, 1874.

During a portion of the past year a very mutinous and insubordinate spirit had prevailed amongst some of the prisoners; their conduct was most violent, and one matron was so grievously assaulted and received such bad treatment, that she was on the sick list for some months.

The description of labour and the hours of employment have been precisely the same as stated in former reports. There has been a great falling off in the orders for shirts by the contractors; consequently, in order to keep the prisoners employed, a large quantity of prison material had to be made up, ready for use when required.

The tailoring department works very well.

The conduct of some of the officers during the year has been satisfactory, whilst that of others has been very unsatisfactory; four were degraded for breach of rules, one dismissed for a very serious neglect of duty, one male officer was discharged in consequence of the infirm state of his health, and two new appointments were made.

The religious instruction of the prisoners has been regularly attended to by the chaplains and lady visitors.

We have to regret the departure from amongst us of the Rev. Dr. Buckeridge, whose untiring zeal and exertions for the reformation of the prisoners cannot be too highly spoken of.

The school continues to be worked in the same satisfactory manner as heretofore.

I have the honour to be, sir,

Your obedient servant,

DELIA J. LIDWILL, Superintendent.

I certify that the rules laid down for the government of the prison have been complied with, except in such cases as have been reported to or brought under the notice of the Director.

DELIA J. LIDWILL, Superintendent.

Captain Barlow,
Director of Convict Prisons,
Dublin Castle.

MOUNTJOY
FEMALE
CONVICT
PRISON.

*Superinten-
dent's
Report.*

RETURN of the NUMBER of CONVICTS received and disposed of
during the year 1874.

					Convicts	Children
In custody, 1st January, 1874,	-	-	-	-	289	4
Received during the year,	-	-	-	-	78	1
Total,	-	-	-	-	367	5
Discharged, sentence completed,	-	-	-	-	13	—
Discharged on licence,	-	-	-	-	18	—
Transferred to lunatic asylum,	-	-	-	-	2	—
Transferred to Refuges, viz.:—Protestant, 3 ; Roman Catholic, 47,	-	-	-	-	50	—
Died, -	-	-	-	-	3	—
Sent to nurse, -	-	-	-	-	—	1
Total disposed of,	-	-	-	86	1
Remaining in custody 31st December, 1874, -	-	-	281	4

AGES OF PRISONERS (ON CONVICTION) NOW IN CUSTODY.		NUMBER OF PRISONERS NOW IN CUSTODY WHO WERE CONVICTED IN THE FOLLOWING YEARS.	
15 years and under 20 years, -	11	In the year, 1851, - - -	1
20 „ 25 „ -	26	„ 1856, - - -	1
25 „ 30 „ -	54	„ 1864, - - -	1
30 „ 35 „ -	50	„ 1865, - - -	1
35 „ 40 „ -	34	„ 1866, - - -	2
40 „ 45 „ -	48	„ 1867, - - -	2
45 years and upwards, -	50	„ 1868, - - -	10
		„ 1869, - - -	12
Total, - -	281	„ 1870, - - -	28
		„ 1871, - - -	45
		„ 1872, - - -	62
Age of oldest prisoner on conviction, 68 years.		„ 1873, - - -	56
		„ 1874, - - -	60
Age of youngest prisoner on conviction, 16 years.		Total, - -	281

SENTENCES of PRISONERS now in CUSTODY.

Transportation—Life,	-	-	2	Penal Servitude—10 years,	-	10
Penal Servitude—Life,	-	-	6	„ 7 „	-	170
„ 20 years,	-	1	„ 5 „	-	90
„ 15 „	-	1			
„ 14 „	-	1	Total,	-	281

CRIMES of PRISONERS now in CUSTODY.

Assault and robbery,	-	3	Larceny from the person,	-	70
Assault with intent to steal from the person,	-	1	Malicious assault,	-	6
Arson,	-	2	Malicious injury to property,	-	1
Burglary and robbery,	-	2	Manslaughter,	-	7
By fraud and force detaining a child under 14 years,	-	1	Milk stealing,	-	2
			Murder,	-	8
Coining,	-	1	Obtaining money under false pretences,	-	1
Felony, and previous conviction,	-	7			
Feloniously wounding,	-	1	Receiving money, knowing it to have been stolen,	-	1
Found concealed on premises at night, with intent to commit felony,	-	1	Receiving stolen goods,	-	3
			Robbery from the person,	-	11
Fowl stealing,	-	1	Robbery with violence,	-	1
Fraudulently obtaining 30 sets of bog oak ornaments,	-	1	Stealing from the person,	-	3
Having base coin in possession,	-	1	Stealing in a dwelling-house £5 and upwards,	-	1
Highway robbery,	-	1	Wounding,	-	1
Larceny,	-	43			
Larceny, and former conviction,	-	90	Total,	-	281

MOUNTJOY
FEMALE
CONVICT
PRISON.
———
Superinten-
dent's
Report.

ESTIMATED VALUE OF PRISONERS' LABOUR for the year ended 31st December, 1874.

How employed.	Average No. of Prisoners employed daily.	Estimated Value of the Work performed.
		£ s. d.
Sewing and knitting prison materials, - -	} 134·06 {	246 7 8
Sewing for customers, 10,768 shirts made, - -		90 2 9
Tailoring, - - - - -	18·83	383 16 1
Washing prison clothing, bedding, &c.,		277 13 8
„ for Mountjoy Male Prison, - - -		146 2 11
„ for Lusk Prison, - - - -	25·35	9 16 4
„ for Government Prisons' Office, -		7 0 8
„ for prison officers, - - -		36 1 9
„ for Royal Irish Constabulary Depôt, - -		109 2 6
Cooking, nursing, cleaning, picking fibre, plaiting, balling, and splicing coir fibre, bone breaking, monitresses in school, for 303 working days, at 8d. per day, - - - - -	74·94	756 17 11
Total, - - - -	253·18	1,953 1 10

Daily average number of prisoners in custody during the year, - 282·670
Per-centage on prison population working, - - - 90·743
„ „ in punishment, - - - 3·895
„ „ sick or infirm, - - - 5·362

MEDICAL OFFICER'S REPORT.

Mountjoy Female Prison,
January, 1875.

SIR,—In forwarding my report of the sanitary condition of this prison for the past year, it affords me much pleasure to be able to state that, notwithstanding the amount of sickness with which we have to deal, the number of deaths in the hospital from all causes during the entire year amounted to but three; one from cancer of the stomach, one from congestion of the lungs, and one from cancer of the womb. There were two convicts transferred to the criminal lunatic asylum at Dundrum for treatment during the year, one of whom (a life prisoner) had been an inmate of the asylum previously, but had been returned as cured. I regret to say that after a year's detention here, it was found necessary to recommend her removal to the asylum again.

The admissions to hospital were 105, as compared with 137 the year before, and the daily average in hospital was twenty. This appears rather a large average, but it should be borne in mind that many infirm and broken-down prisoners who are from time to time admitted, are unavoidably obliged to be retained in the infirm ward in the hospital, as they are unfit for the ordinary work of the prison, or even for the invalid class.

Nothing of an epidemic or contagious nature appeared in the prison, and considering the class from which female convicts are drawn, it is only surprising how well on the whole their health is maintained.

The general health of the staff has been pretty good; twenty matrons were admitted to hospital for treatment, but with a few exceptions, the complaints were of a slight nature, such as colds and catarrhal affections.

In conclusion, I wish to state that Miss M'Carthy, the hospital

matron, has given me every satisfaction in the discharge of her duties
during the year ; and I cannot speak too highly of her unremitting attention to the patients in the hospital.

I have the honour to be, sir,

Your obedient servant,

J. W. YOUNG, M.D., Medical Officer.

To Captain Barlow,
The Director of Convict Prisons.

MOUNTJOY
FEMALE
CONVICT
PRISON.

*Medical
Officer's
Report.*

TABLE 1.—HOSPITAL RETURN for the year 1874.

Number of Prisoners in custody, 1st January, 1874,	289)	367
,, ,, received during the year,	78)	
,, Patients in hospital, 1st January, 1874,	15)	120
,, ,, admitted during the year,	105)	
,, ,, discharged,	93)	
,, ,, died,	3)	120
,, ,, remaining in hospital, 1st January, 1875,	24)	
Daily average of sick in hospital,		20
Externs prescribed for,		1,827
Daily average,		5

TABLE 2.—DEATHS during the year.

Register No.	Initials of Name.	Received in Prison.	Admitted to Hospital.	Date of Death.	Disease.
2054	C. O'N.	6 Nov., 1872,	3 June, 1874,	18 Sept., 1874,	Cancer of stomach.
1995	C. C.	23 Jan., 1872,	8 Oct., 1874,	13 Nov., 1874,	Conjestion of lungs.
1985	A. M'C.	8 Jan., 1872,	15 April, 1874,	25 Nov., 1874,	Cancer of womb.

TABLE 3.—CONVICTS transferred to Dundrum Criminal Lunatic Asylum.

Register No.	Initials of Name.	Where convicted.	Date of conviction.	Removal to Prison.	Sent to Asylum.
2005	M. D.	Wexford,	5 Mar., 1864,	25 June, 1873,	6 June, 1874.
1997	A. W.	Limerick,	11 Jan., 1872,	22 Jan., 1872,	23 June, 1874.

TABLE 4.—DISEASES of those admitted to Hospital.

Sprains,	2	Jaundice,	2
Ulcers,	2	Observation,	7
Old age and debility,	5	Bronchitis,	3
Uterine diseases,	6	Disease of kidneys,	1
Erysipelas,	1	Colic,	3
Febrile affections,	7	Contusion,	1
Abscess,	1	Disease of lungs,	2
Rheumatism,	4	Quinsey,	2
Scrofula,	8	Cutaneous diseases,	3
Dyspepsia and gastric affections,	10	Hysteria,	3
Gumboil,	1	Disease of knee-joint,	1
Pleurisy,	1	Diarrhœa,	5
Catarrh and colds,	20	Fracture of forearm,	1
Boils,	2	Influenza,	2

MOUNTJOY
FEMALE
CONVICT
PRISON.

*Protestant
Chaplain's
Report.*

PROTESTANT CHAPLAIN'S REPORT.

Mountjoy Female Prison,
January, 1875.

Sir,—During the year 1874 I have endeavoured faithfully to discharge the duties incumbent upon me as the Protestant Chaplain of the Mountjoy Female Prison.

The Sunday and Week-day Church Services have been duly celebrated, the Holy Communion has been statedly administered, the prisoners when in hospital, have been visited; one or two of those under my charge, when in punishment, have been carefully attended, and all individually have been conversed with and counselled by me, as it appeared to be advisable.

The Lady Visitors have continued their attendance for the purpose of giving instruction.

This general statement is all that I think it necessary to make, as your supervision of the prison, your constant and minute inspection of my journal, my communication with you personally, or by letter, as circumstances may have required this, leaves me nothing to write by way of a report with which you are not intimately familiar.

I have to acknowledge the courteous attention which my communications have received from you, and I have also the pleasure of acknowledging the prompt and kindly assistance which I have received from the superintendent and other officers of the prison.

Your obedient servant,

DAVID STUART, Protestant Chaplain.

To Captain Barlow,
Director of Convict Prisons,
Dublin Castle.

ROMAN CATHOLIC CHAPLAINS' REPORT.

Mountjoy Female Prison,
February 16th, 1875.

Sir,—In presenting our report for the past year, we are happy to be able to state that the conduct of the vast majority of the prisoners committed to our care has been on the whole very satisfactory. Our duties in the prison have been similar to those of former years, and we observed moreover a singular willingness on the part of the prisoners to avail themselves of the various opportunities afforded them of attending to their religious duties. With a very few exceptions, they approached the sacrament regularly, and exhibited the most edifying attention in the chapel at mass, prayers, and the instructions which we gave.

Whatever truth there may be in the allegation that religion is often practised in prisons through interested and hypocritical motives, in justice to the female prisoners under our charge, we feel it our duty to state that we have every reason to give them credit for earnestness and sincerity.

While reporting thus favourably of their general conduct during the year, we cannot but express our regret that a few days of the year were marked by acts of insubordination and a display of bad feeling towards one of the principal matrons. Yet, we are of opinion, that these disorders were not so much the result of premeditated malice, as the outcome of temporary excitement produced by erroneous impressions to which an accidental coincidence of circumstances lent, in the eyes of the convicts concerned, a species of colouring.

Believing the offenders to have already received ample punishment, we are glad to understand that they are soon to be released from penal class. It is also most gratifying to perceive a great diminution in the number of persons sentenced to bread and water diet; for we are convinced that punishment, when too common or extended to a long period, loses its efficacy, and may be productive of much harm. Although it must be admitted that to leave delinquents for a time in suspense as to the sentence that awaits them, is in itself often a salutary kind of punishment; yet, from our experience, we are inclined to think that with female convicts any such deferment or delay is rarely beneficial.

We beg to testify our gratitude to you for your constant courtesy towards us, to the clergymen who, with your kind permission, from time to time, assisted us in our labours, as also to the good Sisters of Mercy for their visits and instructions. Our best thanks are also due to the superintendent and other officials for the many services rendered us in the discharge of our duties, especially in our visits to the hospital and penal ward.

We cannot conclude our report without an allusion to the resignation of the Rev. Dr. Buckeridge, whose untiring zeal and energy in the fulfilment of his duties as chaplain, had secured for him a happy influence over the prisoners which we can never hope to attain. All connected with the prison regret his resignation, but we are confident that the good effects of his labours will be long felt among the female convicts of Mountjoy.

We have the honour to be, sir,

Your obedient servants,

BARTH. FITZPATRICK, R.C.C.
MICHAEL WALSH, A.R.C.C.

To Captain Barlow,
Director of Convict Prisons,
Dublin Castle.

PRESBYTERIAN CHAPLAIN'S REPORT.

12, Montpelier-hill, Dublin,
January, 1875.

SIR,—In submitting my report for the past year, I have much pleasure in bearing testimony to the uniform good conduct of the prisoners who are under my care. In no one instance has fault been found. Their attention to my Sabbath exercises is pleasingly marked; and the week-day instructions are looked forward to, and regarded as entertaining us well as improving.

To the case of one, A. B., I would respectfully ask the special notice of the authorities. Her crime was truly great; but nineteen years is a long time to be in penal servitude. During all that time her conduct has been without reproach; I believe there is not one mark against her. She gained the good opinion of my predecessor, who used some efforts to procure her freedom. I believe that she is a sincere penitent, and that good would be done to her, and no evil could result to society by holding out the prospect of liberty on the completion of her twentieth year of confinement.

Every facility is given for carrying out the discipline of the prisons

(margin notes:) MOUNTJOY FEMALE CONVICT PRISON. Roman Catholic Chaplains' Report.

(margin note:) Presbyterian Chaplain's Report.

MOUNTJOY FEMALE CONVICT PRISON. for the reformation of criminals. There is no injudicious kindness—certainly there is no unnecessary severity in dealing with the poor creatures, whom it is a duty to aid and a blessedness to save.

Presbyterian Chaplain's Report. I avail myself of the opportunity to express my unqualified satisfaction with the manner in which all officers have discharged their duties, from the active, intelligent, and kind superintendent to the most inexperienced matron.

During the year I have, without interruption, performed Divine service on each Lord's day, and given religious instruction, and conducted devotional exercises on every Tuesday.

I am, sir, yours faithfully,

S. G. MORRISON, Presbyterian Chaplain.

Captain Barlow,
Director of Convict Prisons,
Dublin Castle.

Schoolmistress's Report.

SCHOOLMISTRESS'S REPORT.

Mountjoy Female Prison,
15th January, 1875.

SIR,—I have the honour of submitting my report upon the educational department of this prison for the year ended 31st December, 1874.

The daily average attendance during the year was 158, and 68 prisoners were newly admitted during the same period. Of the latter, 6 were able to read and write well, 12 could read and write indifferently, 16 could read imperfectly but not write, while the remaining 34 were wholly illiterate.

The general management of the school and the mode of instruction pursued have been the same as detailed in previous reports, and both have been carried out with satisfactory results during the year just closed. During that time 15 prisoners were promoted from the first to the second book, 24 from the second to the third, and 29 from the third to the fourth, or highest reading book used in the school. Nearly all evince an anxiety to learn to read, but the teachers observe a strong tendency on the part of prisoners to endeavour to repeat, as it were, by rote, making scarcely any effort to understand what they read. The teachers guard against this by frequent interrogation on the subject-matter of the lesson, and satisfy themselves that the reading conveys something to the minds of the prisoners who, in proportion as they understand what they read, take a greater interest in the instruction imparted to them. There are at present in the prison 104 prisoners able to read, who, on admission, were utterly ignorant.

The progress in writing has also been satisfactory, 76 prisoners being now able to write, who, on admission, were unable to do so. The prisoners begin to learn to write when they are making their first steps in reading the second book, a system which I have found to work well, as the progress they make in the one subject assists their progress in the other, or, as has been well observed, "they are taught to read by writing and to write by reading."

Writing on slates from dictation is also taught, and proves a very profitable occupation. For this purpose, sentences are selected, illustrating some moral truth, or conveying some useful information, and in this way the words are fixed upon the memory, and a favourable impression produced on the mind.

In arithmetic the improvement has been fair, 128 prisoners having learned the principles of notation and numeration, to write down numbers correctly, and to work sums in the simple rules with accuracy and quickness. They are also exercised occasionally by questions in mental arithmetic. Geography is taught from maps, and incidentally from the lessons in the reading books which treat of this subject, and always proves very attractive and instructive to prisoners. MOUNTJOY FEMALE CONVICT PRISON. School-mistress's Report.

Besides the subjects already enumerated, such varied information is given as may be useful to prisoners; for instance, on things which concern them at present, and which will be likely to affect them hereafter; also such advice as will assist them in the performance of their several duties, and encourage them in the practice of industry, good conduct, and obedience to, and respect for, those placed in authority over them. Such advice, I am glad to say, has been received with cheerful attention and earnest thankfulness by the prisoners, and I am led to hope, sir, has had a beneficial effect on many of them.

Forty-seven prisoners were transferred to the refuges during the year. Twenty-eight of these were able to read and write well, 15 could read but none write, and only 4 were unable to either read or write. These latter were women of weak intellect, or defective sight, and though quiet and attentive in school were, for the reasons stated, incapable of making the required proficiency, and on my so certifying, you kindly allowed them the privilege of joining the refuges.

The conduct of the prisoners while under instruction has, with few exceptions, been very satisfactory. They have shown an earnest desire to acquit themselves to the satisfaction of the teachers, and have always been respectful in their conduct and demeanour in school. When it is remembered how few of them have been trained to habits of regularity and submission to authority, and that the most violent and refractory, from time to time, attend school, an occasional act of misconduct may be expected from characters of such antecedents. Such misconduct is always punished by expelling the offender from school for such time as you may decide. The few who had been expelled during the year were, at their own earnest entreaty, and promise of future good conduct, again allowed to attend after the period for which they had been expelled had terminated; and in almost every case those prisoners have shown by their assiduous attention and obedience to the teachers, that they set a proper value on the privilege they had forfeited by their misconduct.

In conclusion, sir, I feel great pleasure in acknowledging the zealous and efficient co-operation I have received from the other teachers during the year.

I have the honour to be, sir,

Your most obedient servant,

MARY DWYER, Head Schoolmistress.

Captain Barlow, &c., &c., &c.,
    Director of Convict Prisons,
        Dublin Castle.

LUSK INTERMEDIATE PRISON.

LUSK
INTERME-
DIATE
PRISON.

——

*Director's
Report.*

No change has taken place in the working of this prison during the past year. The daily average of convicts in custody was 33. One escape took place during the year; the convict has not yet been re-arrested. Having inquired into the case I do not consider blame is to be attributed to the officers of the prison. Nearly three years had elapsed since an escape or attempt at escape had taken place previously.

During the year 67 prisoners were received, 58 were released on licence, 4 were removed for misconduct to other prisons. The conduct and industry of the convicts has been satisfactory.

The management of the prison and farm has been very satisfactory, as has been also the conduct of the staff generally.

That portion of the farm hitherto not partially drained has been now thoroughly drained. The crops, with the exception of the hay crop, were good. The care which has been taken with the land at a considerable outlay promises a remunerative return for years to come. The unavoidable employment of the convicts on the farm has prevented the proper extension of the work at the quarry. I trust, however, this year to place a small party permanently at quarry work.

The buildings have been kept in repair; some of the farm offices have been much improved. A stone building to replace one of the iron huts has been commenced and will be completed next summer.

During the past and preceding year some young cattle have been reared and some purchased. This will for some years to come prevent considerable expense in the purchase of cattle for dairy purposes and feeding. Considering this fact, and the great improvements which have been effected by proper tillage, &c., an increase in the receipts of the farm may be reasonably expected.

The health of both officers and prisoners has been good; but the exposed situation of the farm, together with the severe nature of a considerable portion of the labour at which the convicts are at times placed, has rendered it necessary to remove some cases for a short period to the hospital of Mountjoy Male Convict Prison.

The school has been carried on as in former years.

The agent for discharged convicts has given every assistance to convicts discharged from this and other prisons.

The usual reports and statistics are appended.

J. BARLOW, *Director.*

SUPERINTENDENT'S REPORT.

Lusk Convict Prison,
16th January, 1875.

SIR,—I beg leave to submit the usual annual report on this prison for the year ending 31st December, 1874.

I have little to add to my last and former reports, the duties of the prison being in every particular carried out in the same way.

There has been no change on the staff of officers, and each has discharged his duties very satisfactorily. The conduct and industry of the convicts has been very good, and I have found them willing to work at times when their work was slavish and disagreeable, making drains, &c., during the winter months. Some very handy good workmen, who learned the mason-work at Spike Island, have been employed building a dormitory for themselves, and also one for the warders, and a very good stone building is being raised ; the stones have been found on the farm. Several hundred tons of stones have been raised out of the quarry for buildings, road-making, and drain-work, and some have been sold to the public. Twelve acres of the farm not before fully drained is being made perfect. The works of the farm have been well attended to, and a fair average return of crops. Sixty-seven convicts have been received during the year ; 58 have been released on licence, three of which have been revoked for breaches thereof, 1 has been on commutation of sentence discharged, and 1 without a licence, 4 have been removed for misconduct, and 1 absconded ; the daily average number in custody 33. I beg to suggest that in future a return of the quantities of farm produce, with the stock of cattle, &c., be annexed to report to show what has been done during the year on the farm by convict labour. The usual statistical returns are annexed.

I certify that the rules of the prison have been complied with, and every infringement reported or brought under the notice of the Visiting Director.

I have the honour to be, sir,

Your most obedient servant,

R. GUNNING, Superintendent.

Captain Barlow,
Director, Convict Prisons, Ireland.

RETURN showing the different Crops of the Farm in the year 1874.

	Acres.		Acres.
Meadow,	20	Mangolds,	4
Pasture,	73	Parsnips,	1
Wheat,	18	Carrots,	1
Oats,	32	Peas,	½
Vetches,	2	Beans,	½
Rape,	1	Cabbage,	2
Potatoes,	10	Other garden vegetables,	1
Turnips,	12		

RETURN of Stock of Cattle, Sheep, &c., at Lusk Prison 31st December, 1874.

	No.		No.
Stall feeding,	23	Rams,	2
Cows,	9	Working horses,	5
Two years old,	4	Young horses,	4
One year old,	6	Asses,	1
Calves,	7	Bulls,	1
Sheep ewes,	65	Pigs,	54

LUSK
INTERME-
DIATE
PRISON.

*Superinten-
dent's
Report.*

RETURN showing the Number of Convicts in custody during the year ended 31st December, 1874, and how they have been disposed of.

In custody 1st January, 1874,	38
Received from Mountjoy Male Convict Prison,	2
„ from Spike Island *via* Mountjoy,	65
Total,	**105**
Released on licence,	58
Discharged on commutation of sentence,	1
„ on completion of period of penal servitude equal to time unexpired when licence was granted,	1
Removed to Mountjoy Male Prison Hospital,	3
„ „ for misconduct,	4
Absconded,	1
	70
Remaining in custody, 31st December, 1874,	35
Total,	**105**
Daily average number in custody,	33

ACCOUNT showing the value of Productive Labour of Prisoners at Lusk for the year ended 31st December, 1874.

Trades.	Amount.	Observations.
	£ s. d.	
Tailoring,	23 16 0	
Shoemaking,	18 4 0	
Carpenters,	65 10 0	
Masons,	41 0 0	Daily average number, - 33
Smiths,	15 0 0	Less sick, - ·42
	163 10 0	32·58
Thirty prisoners employed at general farm work for fifty-two weeks, at 11s. a week,	858 0 0	Average earning of each effective prisoner, £31 7s. 1d.
Total,	**1,021 10 0**	

RETURN showing the Proportion of Sick and Deaths to the number of Prisoners in this Prison for the year ended 31st December, 1874.

Daily Average No. of Prisoners.	Daily Average No. of Sick.	No. of Deaths.	Per-centage on Prison Population.
33	·42	~	-

SENTENCES of 67 Convicts received during the year ended 31st December, 1874.

5 years' penal servitude,	37
7 „ „	26
10 „ „	3
20 „ „	1
Total,	**67**

LUSK
INTERMEDIATE
PRISON.

*Superinten-
dent's
Report.*

AGES on reception of 67 Convicts received during the year.

20 years and under 30,	- - - - - -	27
30 ,, ,, 40,	- - - - - -	27
40 ,, ,, 50,	- - - - - -	10
50 ,, ,, 60,	- - - - - -	1
60 years and upwards,	- - - - - -	2
	Total, - - - -	67

CRIMES of 67 Convicts received during the year.

Army offences, - - - - - - - -	2
Assault, - - - - - - - - -	1
,, grevious, - - - - - - -	1
,, and robbery, - - - - - -	1
,, with intent to maim, - - - -	1
,, under statute, - - - - -	1
Burglary, - - - - - - - -	3
,, and robbery, - - - - - -	4
Breaking and entering shop and stealing therein, -	1
,, into dwelling and stealing therein, - -	2
Cattle-stealing, - - - - - - -	4
Child desertion, - - - - - - -	1
Coining, - - - - - - - -	1
Forgery, - - - - - - - -	1
Feloniously stealing goods, - - - - -	1
Highway robbery, - - - - - -	1
Housebreaking, and larceny, - - - -	2
,, ,, robbery, - - - -	1
Larceny, - - - - - - - -	6
,, from person, - - - - -	7
,, of goods, - - - - - -	1
,, and previous conviction, - - -	6
,, money from person, - - -	1
,, horse, saddle, winkers, &c., - -	1
Rape, - - - - - - - -	2
Robbery, - - - - - - - -	1
,, with violence, - - - - -	1
Receiving and former conviction, - - - -	2
Sacrilege, - - - - - - - -	1
Sheep-stealing, - - - - - - -	5
Stealing hens after previous conviction for felony, -	1
Stealing Post letters, - - - - - -	1
Obtaining money under false pretences, - -	1
House robbery and former felony, - - -	1
Total, - - -	67

RETURN showing the reported Previous Convictions of 67 Convicts received during the year ended 31st December, 1874.

Not reported to have been in Prison before, - -	15
Once, - - - - - - - -	19
Twice, - - - - - - - -	6
Three times, - - - - - - -	5
Four ,, - - - - - - -	7
Five ,, - - - - - - -	4
Six ,, - - - - - - -	3
Eight ,, - - - - - - -	2
Ten ,, - - - - - - -	2
Twenty-six times, - - - - - -	1
Thirty-three ,, - - - - - -	1
Forty-three ,, - - - - - -	1
Fifty-four ,, - - - - - -	1
Total, - - - -	67

Of the above number 14 served in the army.

PROTESTANT CHAPLAIN'S REPORT.

Lusk, January 7, 1875.

Protestant Chaplain's Report.

SIR,—I have not observed any circumstances connected with the Protestant convicts who have been received into Lusk Intermediate Prison during last year, and who have attended my instructions in the prison, which would render it necessary for me to lay before you a long report. With two exceptions their conduct has been very good, and the prospect of soon regaining their liberty, as well as the kind treatment they receive from the officials, compensate for the necessary strictness of prison rules. Indeed, I have not failed to point out, if any should be disposed to grumble at the discipline and system of the prison life, how favourably they are now circumstanced, and how convict prison discipline now (as reformed in accordance with modern ideas), compared with the old system, which brought the scourge, the manacle, and the fetters into almost daily use, and rarely afforded any means of deliverance from the felon's cell, except that which was provided by the gallows or expatriation to a penal settlement in some remote and blighted land from which the exile never could hope to return. I find my class very attentive in Church and to the weekly devotional exercises in the prison, but as a general rule they are reserved and reluctant to speak much ever on religious matters, and I am often at a loss to know whether this proceeds from unwillingness or inability to answer my inquiries. However, on the whole, I would pronounce them hopeful men. With the exception of the Holy Communion they join in every other part of their religious duties with relish, and I hope with profit.

I continue to receive every attention and assistance from the Superintendent and the warders, and have the honour to remain,

Your obedient servant,

RICHARD WRIGHTSON, Protestant Chaplain.

To Captain Barlow,
Director of Convict Prisons, Ireland.

ROMAN CATHOLIC CHAPLAIN'S REPORT.

Lusk, January, 1875.

GENTLEMEN,—My report for the year 1874 is but the repetition of the reports of former years. It is indeed gratifying to be able, year after year, to bear willing testimony to the good order and regularity with which the prison duties are performed, to the zeal and efficiency of the officers, as also to the good will exhibited by the prisoners in the discharge of their allotted tasks.

I am, gentlemen, your obedient servant,

N. O'FARRELL, P.P.

MEDICAL OFFICER'S REPORT.

LUSK
INTERME-
DIATE
PRISON.

Lusk Government Prison,
1st January, 1875.

*Medical
Officer's
Report.*

SIR,—I beg to submit the usual annual report of the sanitary condition of this prison during the past year.

The health of the prisoners has been excellent during that period. This has required a good deal of watchful care, owing to the circumstances that the average physical strength of the prisoners confined here during the past year has not been equal to that of former years. Mr. Gunning, the Superintendent, and the other officers have devoted great care and attention to the diet, clothing, and general comfort of the prisoners. The new stone building which you are erecting will greatly conduce to their health.

The health of the officers and their families has been excellent during the past year.

I observe with great satisfaction that you have maintained the standard of dietary and clothing of the prisoners. This is in reality an economy, inasmuch as it prevents the expenditure and loss which would be entailed by the illness which would be caused by a less liberal scale. The work of the prisoners in making drains is arduous, and in wet weather especially so. The physical condition of the prisoners, as described in the beginning of my report, makes good diet and clothing more than ever necessary.

I am, sir, your obedient servant,

FRANCIS J. B. QUINLAN, M.D., T.C.D.

Medical Superintendent.

To the Director of Government Prisons.

REGISTRAR AND SCHOOL INSTRUCTOR'S REPORT.

*Registrar
and School
Instructor's
Report.*

Lusk Convict Prison,
19th January, 1875.

SIR,—I beg leave to submit the following report on the educational department of this prison for the year ending 31st December, 1874.

On the 1st January there were in the prison 38 convicts, all of whom attended school, admitted during the year 67 convicts, making a total of 105 inmates within the year. Of these 60 were discharged and 10 disposed of by removal to Mountjoy Male Prison for hospital treatment, &c., leaving 35 prisoners attending school on the 31st December, 1874. The report on the school of this prison for each succeeding year is necessarily a reiteration of the one that preceded it, and no change has taken place either in the mode of instruction or the hours of attendance. The convicts have been most attentive to the instructions given them; their conduct and demeanour in school unexceptionally good, and so well have they availed themselves of the opportunities for improving in reading, writing, &c., afforded them in the other prisons and in this, that almost all the prisoners discharged from this prison during the year could read and write, the exceptions being the ordinary class of old men.

I am, sir, your most obedient servant,

CHARLES DALY,

School Instructor, &c.

To Captain Barlow,
Director of Convict Prisons,
Dublin Castle.

APPENDIX.

RETURN showing the PROPORTION of SICK and DEATHS to the Number of Prisoners in the Irish Convict Prisons for the years 1854, 1855, 1856, 1857, 1858, and 1859.

	1854.					1855.				
—	Spike Island and Phillipstown.	Cork and Grangegorman.	Newgate and Smithfield.	Mountjoy.	Totals, 1854.	Spike Island and Phillipstown.	Cork and Grangegorman.	Newgate and Smithfield.	Mountjoy.	Totals, 1855.
No. of Prisoners, .	2,290	339	556	443	3,628	1,777	488	430	452	3,147
Average daily No. of Sick, . .	276	25	46	21	368	203	36	65	17	321
No. of Deaths, .	241	6	33	9	289	101	8	31	9	149
Per-centage on prison population, .	10·5	1·8	5·9	2·	8·	5·7	1·6	7·2	2·	4·7

	1856.					1857.				
—	Spike Island and Phillipstown.	Cork and Grangegorman.	Newgate and Smithfield.	Mountjoy.	Totals, 1856.	Spike Island and Phillipstown.	Cork, Grangegorman, and Newgate.	Smithfield and Lusk.	Mountjoy.	Totals, 1857.
No. of Prisoners, .	1,619	613	199	421	2,852	1,329	686	70	357	2,442
Average daily No. of Sick, . .	101	42	35	16	194	67	37	6	16	126
No. of Deaths, .	35	11	5	8	54	34	6	2	3	45
Per-centage on prison population, .	2·1	1·8	2·5	·7	1·9	2·6	·9	2·9	·8	1·8

	1858.					1859.				
—	Spike Island and Phillipstown.	Female Prisons.	Smithfield and Lusk.	Mountjoy Male.	Totals, 1858.	Spike Island and Phillipstown.	Mountjoy Female.	Smithfield and Lusk.	Mountjoy Male.	Totals, 1859.
No. of Prisoners, .	1,003	593	97	320	2,013	837	464	99	293	1,693
Average daily No. of Sick, . .	41	41	4	12	98	32	14	8	13	62
No. of Deaths, .	16	12	2	3	33	11	3	—	1	15
Per-centage on prison population,	1·6	2·	3·6	0·9	1·6	1·3	0·6	—	0·3	0·9

RETURN showing the PROPORTION of SICK and DEATHS to the APPENDIX. Number of Prisoners in the Irish Convict Prisons for the years 1860, 1861, 1862, 1863, 1864, and 1865.

—	1860.					1861.				
	Spike Island and Philipstown.	Mountjoy Female.	Smithfield and Lusk.	Mountjoy Male.	Totals, 1860.	Spike Island and Philipstown.	Mountjoy Female.	Smithfield and Lusk.	Mountjoy Male.	Totals, 1861.
No. of Prisoners, .	703	423	105	251	1,563	676	394	94	205	1,369
Average daily No. of Sick, . .	22	17	4	11	54	15	20	4	11	50
No. of Deaths, .	3	11	—	1	15	1	6	1	3	11
Per-centage on prison population, .	·3	2·6	—	·4	·96	·1	1·5	1·1	1·5	·80

—	1862.					1863.				
	Spike Island and Philipstown *	Mountjoy Female.	Smithfield and Lusk.	Mountjoy Male.	Totals, 1862.	Spike Island.	Mountjoy Female.	Smithfield and Lusk.	Mountjoy Male.	Totals, 1863.
No. of Prisoners, .	700	416	79	316	1,519	783	460	75	370	1,688
Average daily No. of Sick, . .	14	37	4	17	62	9	26	4	17	56
No. of Deaths, .	8	10	—	5	23	10	4	—	5	19
Per-centage on prison population, .	1·1	2·4	—	1·5	1·5	1·3	·8	—	1·3	1·1

—	1864.					1865.				
	Spike Island.	Mountjoy Female.	Smithfield and Lusk.	Mountjoy Male.	Totals, 1864.	Spike Island.	Mountjoy Female.	Smithfield and Lusk.	Mountjoy Male.	Totals, 1865.
No. of Prisoners, .	918	499	99	290	1,806	901	486	105	221	1,713
Average daily No. of Sick, . .	8	30	8	16	62	8	28	5	19	60
No. of Deaths, .	7	13	2	10	32	10	10	2	2	24
Per-centage on prison population, .	·7	2·6	2·0	3·4	1·7	1·1	·2	1·9	·9	1·4

* Philipstown Prison was closed on the 31st March, 1852.

RETURN showing the PROPORTION of SICK and DEATHS to the Number of Prisoners in the Irish Convict Prisons for the years 1866, 1867, 1868, 1869, and 1870.

1866.

—	Spike Island.	Mountjoy Female.	Smithfield and Lusk.	Mountjoy Male.	Total, 1866.
No. of Prisoners,	799	462	96	191	1,548
Average daily No. of Sick,	12	23	3	10	48
No. of Deaths,	12	5	–	6	23
Per-centage on prison population,	1·5	1· ·	– –	3·1	1·4

1867.

—	Spike Island.	Mountjoy Female.	Smithfield and Lusk.	Mountjoy Male.	Total, 1867.
No. of Prisoners,	722	426	80	159	1,387
Average daily No. of Sick,	12	24	3	8	47
No. of Deaths,	9	3	–	1	13
Per-centage on prison population,	1·2	·7	–	·6	·9

1868.

—	Spike Island.	Mountjoy Female.	Smithfield and Lusk.	Mountjoy Male.	Total, 1868.
No. of Prisoners,	696	409	74	154	1,333
Average daily No. of Sick,	12	24	3	3	42
No. of Deaths,	8	5	–	1	14
Per-centage on prison population,	1·1	1·2	–	·6	1

1869.

—	Spike Island.	Mountjoy Female.	Smithfield* and Lusk.	Mountjoy Male.	Total, 1869.
No. of Prisoners,	663	369	81	144	1,296
Average daily No. of Sick,	13	23	3	3	40
No. of Deaths,	3	7	–	·1	11
Per-centage on prison population,	·4	1·7	–	·8	·8

1870.

—	Spike Island.	Mountjoy Female.	Lusk.	Mountjoy Male.	Total, 1870.
No. of Prisoners,	675	340	61	157	1,233
Average daily No. of Sick,	13	19	·6	4	38 6
No. of Deaths,	2	6	1	–	9
Per-centage on prison population,	·2	1·7	1 5	–	·7

* Smithfield Prison was closed and the Prisoners transferred to Lusk on 15th June, 1869.

RETURN showing the PROPORTION of SICK and DEATHS to the APPENDIX.
Number of Prisoners in the Irish Convict Prisons for the years
1871, 1872, 1873, and 1874.

1871.

—	Spike Island.	Mountjoy Female.	Lusk.	Mountjoy Male.	Total, 1871.
No. of Prisoners, . . .	694	383	61	135	1,223
Average daily No. of Sick, .	.11	22	·2	3	8C·2
No. of Deaths, ...	4	5	–	1	10
Per-centage on prison population.	·5	1·4	–	·7	·8

1872.

—	Spike Island.	Mountjoy Female.	Lusk.	Mountjoy Male.	Total, 1872.
No. of Prisoners, . . .	664	320	57	131	1,172
Average daily No. of Sick, .	13	15	·4	3	31·4
No. of Deaths, . . .	8	5	–	–	13
Per-contage on prison population,	1·2	1·5	–	–	1·1

1873.

—	Spike Island.	Mountjoy Female.	Lusk.	Mountjoy Male.	Total, 1873.
No. of Prisoners, . . .	640	299	45	145	1,129
Average daily No. of Sick, .	11	13	·2	6	30·2
No. of Deaths, . . .	8	5	–	1	14
Per-contage on prison population,	1·2	1·6	–	·6	1·2

1874.

—	Spike Island.	Mountjoy Female.	Lusk.	Mountjoy Male.	Total, 1874.
No. of Prisoners, . . .	664	283	33	154	1,133
Average daily No. of Sick, .	13	13	·4	5	31·4
No. of Deaths, . . .	7	3	–	1	11
Per-contage on prison population,	1·0	1·0	–	·6	·9

RETURN showing the EXPENDITURE under each HEAD of SERVICE in the year ended 31st March, 1874, made by the DIRECTOR of CONVICT PRISONS.

Heads of Service.	Total 1,130.	Mountjoy, 151 Males.	Mountjoy, 295 Females.	Lusk, 40 Males.	Spike Island, 644 Males.
	£ s. d.	£ s. d.	£ s. d.	£ s. d.	£ s. d.
COST OF STAFF.					
Salaries and wages,	13,519 17 4	3,112 7 6	2,742 17 6	750 9 10	6,914 4 6
Allowance in lieu of rations and quarters,	1,703 8 9	328 0 1	438 5 3	81 19 4	845 4 1
Uniform for officers,	931 6 11	191 11 9	147 17 6	70 0 5	512 17 3
Total cost of staff,	16,154 13 0	3,631 19 4	3,329 0 3	901 9 7	8,272 8 10
Annual cost per prisoner,	14 5 11	24 1 6	11 5 8	22 0 8	12 18 10
MAINTENANCE OF CONVICTS.					
Victualling for convicts, including medical comforts for sick,	11,256 6 4	1,563 6 11	2,990 5 5	596 6 5	6,107 7 7
Medicines, surgical instruments, &c.,	171 8 2	58 4 1	45 0 9	3 13 6	64 9 10
Soap scouring and cleaning articles,	442 10 3	86 4 0	190 17 2	10 1 6	144 7 7
Clothing for prisoners,*	2,895 5 7	545 3 2	434 1 8	327 6 9	1,285 14 0
Fuel and light,†	4,863 0 2	1,503 11 2	1,076 17 1	146 16 0	1,838 15 11
Total expenses of maintenance,	19,058 10 6	3,761 9 4	4,737 2 1	1,014 4 2	9,525 14 11
Annual cost per prisoner,	16 10 3	24 18 2	16 2 6	25 7 1	14 15 10
Bedding for prisoners,	26 7 10	0 4 4	15 11 6	—	12 12 0
Furniture and fittings,†	207 3 1	82 15 8	62 5 6	2 6 0	20 13 11
Kitchen utensils, crockery, &c.,	83 2 11	10 2 1	20 4 1	1 16 9	—
Escort and conveyance of convicts,	149 14 8	11 17 1	42 13 10	42 3 4	53 0 5
Gratuities to convicts,	1,542 6 6	11 9 6	1466 13 10	675 12 7	388 10 7
Ordinary repairs of buildings,†	3,463 9 4	678 9 11	603 18 7	32 2 2	2,186 18 9
Rents, rates, and taxes,†	189 0 8	45 6 5	90 16 11	2 14 11	—
Incidental expenses,	354 3 4	84 7 4	131 2 3	31 0 0	117 18 9
Gross total expenses,	41,069 16 5	8,218 3 0	9,539 8 8	2,723 11 6	20,586 13 1
Gross annual charge per prisoner,	36 6 11	54 8 6	32 3 8	68 1 9	30 5 3
DEDUCT—					
Value of labour, exclusive of employments in the service of the prison,§	15,067 0 5	1,120 13 9	1,576 11 5	1,132 6 0	11,287 10 3
Incidental receipts (sale of old stores, &c.),	163 15 0	3 9 4	64 17 4	15 4 8	90 3 8
Total deductions,	15,230 15 5	1,124 2 1	1,641 8 9	1,147 10 8	11,317 13 11
Net cost (with the above deductions)	25,839 1 0	7,094 0 11	7,897 19 11	1,576 0 10	9,270 19 2
Net annual charge per prisoner (do.)	22 17 4	46 19 7	26 15 5	80 8 5	14 7 11

* This item includes the cost of clothing supplied to prisoners on liberation, which amounted to £507 11s. 4d., viz.:—£4 8s. 8d., in Mountjoy Male Convict Prison; £150 11s. 3d., in Mountjoy Female Convict Prison; £213 1s. 1d., in Lusk Prison; and £139 10s. 4d., in Spike Island Prison.

† The expenditure under these heads of service is defrayed by the Board of Public Works, and the amounts shown have been furnished by that department.

‡ This amount includes the gratuities earned by Female Convicts while on licence in refuges.

§ This sum includes the gratuities earned by the Convicts while in the other prisons before their removal to Lusk.

‖ Owing to a very considerable amount of the labour of the Convicts being under the control of other departments, it is not possible to make a calculation based on measurements; the value of labour given in the return has been based on a daily rate of wages calculated at about one-third less than that paid to tradesmen and labourers in the localities where the prisons are situated; as the works on which Convicts are employed are principally for Government, only a small portion of the amount set down is actually received in cash.

www.ingramcontent.com/pod-product-compliance
Lightning Source LLC
Chambersburg PA
CBHW032033090426
42733CB00031B/957

* 9 7 8 3 7 4 1 1 0 5 2 4 1 *